The Tech Contracts
HANDBOOK

Software Licenses and Technology Services Agreements for Lawyers and Businesspeople

David W. Tollen

Section of
Intellectual Property Law

AMERICAN BAR ASSOCIATION

Cover by ABA Publishing

Printed in the United States of America

Library of Congress Cataloging-in-Publication Data

Tollen, David W.
   The tech contracts handbook : software licenses and technology services agreements for businesspeople and lawyers / David W. Tollen.
      p. cm.
   Includes bibliographical references and index.
   ISBN 978-1-60442-982-4
   1. Computer contracts—United States.   2. Technology transfer—Law and legislation—United States.   3. License agreements—United States.   4. Computer software—Licenses—United States.   5. Copyright—Computer programs—United States.   I. Title.
   KF905.C6T65   2010
   346.7302—dc22

                                                                        2010021468

14 13 12 11   5 4

Thank you to my wife, Wendy Pagett-Tollen. Thanks also to Mani Adeli, Paul Ambrosio, Jay Botelho, Lee Bruno, Michael C. Carlson, Ralph Chandler, H. Ward Classen, Christopher B. Conner, Matteo Daste, Gary S. Davis, Mark K. Dickson, R. Oak Dowling, Roxanna Friedrich, Frederick Gault Jr., Kim David Greenwood, Jennifer Hanley, Michael A. Jacobs, Nels Johnson, John M. Keagy, Michael F. Kelleher, Cecilia Toman Mangoba, Alex Mann, Nathaniel D. McKitterick, Denise Olrich, Kathy O'Sullivan, Martin Plack, Robert A. Preskill, Mark F. Radcliffe, Ian A. Rambarran, Michelle M. Reichert, Ken Stratton, Robert W. Tollen, Larry Townsend, Richard Vestuto, and Amy Ward.

Please visit **www.TechContractsHandbook.com**
*for contract clauses and forms you can download and
for other resources.*

Contents

About the Author

Attorney David W. Tollen has served as General Counsel of a publicly traded software company, as Vice President of Business Development for a technology start-up, and as a lawyer in a Silicon Valley practice. He graduated with honors from Harvard Law School and has degrees from Cambridge University in England and U.C. Berkeley. Mr. Tollen began his practice at a global law firm and went on to cofound Adeli & Tollen LLP (www.AdeliTollen.com), a technology and intellectual property firm with offices in San Francisco, Los Angeles, and Mountain View. His practice focuses on information technology and intellectual property transactions, including software licensing, as well as Internet and e-commerce law. He is also the founder of Tech Contracts Chalkboard (www.TechContracts.com), which provides training on drafting and negotiating technology agreements for both lawyers and businesspeople. He lives and works in the San Francisco Bay Area.

Introduction

This book will help you negotiate, draft, and understand information technology contracts. Specifically, it will help you with software licenses and other software transfers, as well as technology services agreements. It addresses contracts between businesses, as well as business-to-consumer and business-to-government contracts. It also addresses both Internet-related and offline contracts.

This book is for both lawyers and nonlawyers. The text doesn't use any technical jargon—any "legalese," "engineerese," or "programmerese." It's written in simple English, like a good contract.

You can use this book as a training manual or a reference guide or both. If you're training, read this book cover to cover. It provides an overview of the key technology contracting concepts.

If you're after a reference guide, you can pick and choose the chapters to read. When you're negotiating a contract, or reading or writing one, look up the various clauses to learn what they mean and what's at stake. You'll find sample language in each chapter, which you can incorporate into your own contracts. Plus, if you visit this book's website,[1] you can copy the longer sample clauses and paste them into your document. You can also use this book's table of contents as an issue spotter: as a checklist of clauses to consider.

Finally, you can use this book as a source of full-length contract forms. Appendix 1 provides a printed contract form, and this book's website offers that form and several others in electronic format. See Appendix 1 for a list of the contracts available. Or see the website itself.

This book can't replace a lawyer—or a colleague with more information technology (IT) experience, if you are a lawyer. But it can help you understand your lawyer—or colleague. And whether you

---

1. www.TechContractsHandbook.com.

have legal help or not, the better you understand your contracts, the more effective you'll be.

I'm a technology lawyer, and this book grew out of a seminar I teach, for both attorneys and nonattorneys. At the end of the program, students often asked where they could learn more—if there was a good book on software and IT services contracts. Most of the books I knew were massive tomes on intellectual property or contract law. They're written for lawyers only, and their more practical lessons are spread across hundreds or thousands of pages. I've learned much of my trade on the job, rather than from a book. I've served as a technology lawyer with a global firm, as general counsel for a publicly traded software company, and as vice president of business development for an Internet start-up. I now practice through my own technology-focused law firm in San Francisco and the Silicon Valley. The material for my seminar came from the contracts I've negotiated and written in those positions. I'd never seen a really user-friendly outline of the issues. So I wrote this book.

• • • •

The rest of this introduction provides more detail about the types of contracts this book covers. It also offers three lessons about contracting in general. Finally, it explains the structure of a contract and of this book, and it offers a few explanations that will help you get the most out of your reading.

Subject Matter

This book covers (1) software licenses and other software contracts, (2) information technology services contracts, and (3) combination contracts, which include both software and services. The text calls the parties to all these agreements the "provider" and the "recipient."

Software contracts include end user licenses, distribution contracts, assignments, and work-for-hire agreements. In all these deals, the provider transfers intellectual property (IP) rights to the recipient. The IP rights in question usually come from copyright law, though other forms of intellectual property sometimes play a role.[2] The rights transferred might be limited, like the right to copy or dis-

---

2. For a broader explanation of IP and its role in software contracts, see Appendix 2.

tribute software. Or the recipient might receive all IP rights and become the software's new owner.

Services contracts call on the provider to *help* the recipient, rather than to provide software or IP. The provider is going to *do* something. In the information technology industry, that "something" generally has to do with software and computers. IT services include network management, technology maintenance, tech support, system integration, website development, and integrated circuit design, as well as Internet connectivity and software as a service.

Finally, in a combination contract, the provider agrees to provide *both* software and services. Computer programming contracts, for instance, usually call on the provider to write software, a service, and to transfer IP rights in that software. Technology integration agreements often work the same way: the provider licenses or sells software to the recipient and also provides a service by integrating several applications into a computer system. A combination contract works like two contracts in one. It needs terms appropriate for both software and services.

Software and IT services may be delivered via the Internet or via other means. So most of the clauses discussed in this book work for Internet-related agreements and for agreements that have nothing to do with the Internet. However, the Internet and e-commerce raise some unique contracting issues. This book addresses those issues in Appendices 4 and 5.

The provider of software or services is usually a business, but the recipient may be a business or a consumer. The recipient may also be a government agency, and this book should help you understand most government IT contracts. The following text does not, however, address government contracting *rules*, like the federal acquisition regulations (FARs) or the procurement regulations of any state. Some of those rules dictate the language to be inserted in government contracts. This book may not address the exact language required by the rule, but it should help you understand much of the government's language.[3] (And of course, where the government doesn't insist on its own language, you can use the following sample clauses.)

---

3. Some government contracting rules require clauses that aren't specifically related to technology, like "buy American" provisions and clauses on conflicts of interest or use of recycled paper. This book doesn't address those clauses.

Three Lessons about Contracting

1. Good Fences Make Good Neighbors

Why do we sign contracts? It's not because we want to win a lawsuit later. It's not because we don't trust each other. It's not even because we're afraid lawyers will stir up trouble if they're not kept busy.

We sign contracts because good fences make good neighbors.

The best way to avoid arguments in a business relationship is to write down the parties' expectations ahead of time. That list becomes a boundary marker—like a fence between neighboring yards—explaining who's responsible for what. If the parties disagree, they can look at the list for guidance.

In other words, contracts *prevent* disputes—at least, good ones do. They prevent lawsuits.

Even if the parties never look back at the contract once it's signed, it's still probably played a vital role. When people put their business expectations on paper, they often find those expectations don't match. Just the act of negotiating a written[4] contract will uncover many mismatched expectations. The parties can address them before starting work.

Yes, it is true that we sometimes fight over contracts in lawsuits. And yes, in interpreting a contract, we often talk about what a judge would say it means. But that's only because courts have the ultimate say if the parties can't agree. Job No. 1 for the contract is to keep the parties out of court.

2. There Is No Such Thing as "Legalese" or "Technicalese"

You may feel uncomfortable with contracts because of the unfamiliar language they use. Don't be intimidated. You can understand most contracts.

There really is no such thing as legalese. American contracts are written in English (or Spanish or Vietnamese or whatever language

---

4. Many contracts can be oral rather than written, but some can't. And oral contracts have serious disadvantages. Without a clear recording of the terms, the parties have to rely on memories, so the contract won't serve as much of a road map. And oral contracts usually cover only high-level issues, leaving doubt about whether the parties actually agree on vital details.

the parties speak). But contracts do sometimes use special short-hand—terms lawyers have developed to save time. And some IT contracts use "technology shorthand." Finally, contracts sometimes use formal, stilted language with long run-on sentences. Don't let shorthand or stilted language bother you.

If you run into an unfamiliar term in a contract—unfamiliar shorthand—don't worry. Look it up. If it's legal shorthand, you can probably find the definition in a standard dictionary, or online, or in *Black's Law Dictionary*,[5] found in many libraries. Or, better yet, ask a lawyer. Treat technology terms the same way. Look them up in a dictionary or technical manual or online. Or ask someone with the right expertise.

Once you understand a term, feel free to use it in your own contracts. But you should also feel free *not* to use it. Shorthand is optional. If you do use shorthand, be sure the contract defines each technical term. Definitions can vary for IT terms like "RGB" and "bot,"[6] so the contract needs an agreed definition, unless there really can't be any doubt. (See *The Structure of a Contract and of This Book*, page xvi, for more on defined terms.) Legal terms, on the other hand, often have widely accepted definitions, so you usually don't need to define them in the contract.

As for long sentences, just take a deep breath and read slowly. The same goes for formal language. There really is no reason to use terms like "heretofore" and "*ipso facto*." That sort of language often appears in form contracts from the olden days, when formal writing was more popular. It does crop up in modern contracts—often because someone wants to show off a big vocabulary. Be suitably impressed. Then take out your dictionary if necessary and figure out what each sentence says. And avoid terms like that in your own writing.

3. Leverage Is Everything; "Fairness" Is Nothing

A lot of people who negotiate contracts get tied up in knots over what is *fair*. They feel outraged if they're "forced" to sign an "unfair"

---

5. From the West Publishing Company.

6. *RGB*: red-green-blue, a term used for computer screen technology. *Bot*: a software program that mimics human behavior in that it's automated (short for *robot*).

contract. That's a bad way to look at contracts. You'll do better if you think about *leverage*, not fairness.

In general, no one *has* to sign a contract. So if you do agree to terms you dislike, terms that seem "unfair," you probably are getting something worthwhile. Obviously, you're not getting as much as you wanted, but you wouldn't have agreed if the exchange weren't better than nothing—better than not doing business at all. So long as no one's pointing a gun at your head (or otherwise forcing you through illegal "duress"), whatever terms you accept are probably fair.[7]

So if considerations of fairness *aren't* decisive, how do the parties resolve differences of opinion during negotiations? What guides the arguing and negotiating, and the eventual compromise or knuckling under that leads to a contract? It's *leverage*.

If you need the deal more than the other party, you will probably give more. And vice versa. It's that simple. Don't get upset about it, and when you're in the power position, don't take advantage of it too much. You never know when positions will reverse.

The Structure of a Contract and of This Book

Software and services contract terms fall into three groups: transactional clauses, general clauses, and supporting clauses. This book is organized the same way.

The transactional clauses express the deal's central terms. There, the provider grants a license or other rights to software, or promises to provide services—or both. The recipient, on the other hand, promises to pay. This book addresses transactional clauses in Part I.

The general clauses account for most of the rest of the contract. They cover everything not addressed in the transactional clauses or the supporting clauses. This book addresses general clauses in Part II.

Supporting clauses cover the theoretically noncontroversial mechanics of a deal: terms on independent contractor status, contract construction, choice of law, etc. Information technology profession-

---

7. OK, that's not entirely true, at least as far as the law is concerned. There are some terms courts won't enforce because they're "opposed to public policy" or "unconscionable."

als call many of these clauses "boilerplate" and place them at the end of a contract. This book addresses supporting clauses in Part III.

Most contracts start with two sets of supporting clauses: the introduction and recitals and the definitions.[8] From there on, you should organize your clauses the way they're listed: transactional clauses, then general clauses, then the remaining supporting clauses. That makes agreements easy to understand. Unfortunately though, you'll probably find contracts with the clauses jumbled together, in no particular order.

Using This Book

The following five brief notes and explanations will help you get the most out of this book.

First, "one size fits all" rarely works for contracts. Good contracts are customized. So look at this book as a source of *general* lessons to be applied thoughtfully to each deal. Your deal probably raises unique issues. "We don't have an office near Albuquerque, so services there will be delayed." "We can't promise the software will interface with your payroll system because we've never tested it." "Our CFO gets hives if we pay more than twenty percent in advance." This book offers building blocks for a contract addressing issues like those, but the customizations are up to you.

Bear that in mind as you review the example clauses. This book is full of sample contract language, mostly in separate *clause boxes*. If you put one of those clauses into your contract, you will probably need to tweak it.

Second, this book addresses U.S. law. That means it may not be useful for foreign contracts. Within the United States, the fifty states have similar contract laws, and federal law governs some of the issues discussed here. But state laws do vary. Some lessons here apply better to one state than another. That's one of the reasons you should consider help from an experienced lawyer.

Third, like most contracts, the examples in this book use defined terms. When a contract creates a concept and uses it more than once, it usually defines it. For instance, a contract might list the provider's services in Section 2, then mention them over and over in

---

8. See Chapters III.A and III.B.

other sections. Rather than listing the services repeatedly, the contract defines the list as the "Services." Whenever the contract refers to the "Services" with a capital S, it means the whole list. This book's sample clauses work the same way: capitalized words that aren't proper names represent defined terms—e.g., "Software," "Effective Date," "Statement of Work," this "Agreement." (Some contracts mark defined terms with all caps instead—e.g., the "SERVICES.") The same goes for sets of initials in all caps, like "NDA" (for nondisclosure agreement). In this book, the sample clause often won't supply the definition. That's because, in a real contract, that term would be defined in another section. Obviously, in your contracts, you should provide the definitions somewhere. For more on defined terms, see Chapter III.B.

Fourth, almost all the sample clauses use the defined terms "Provider" and "Recipient." As noted, the text refers to the contracting parties the same way. Don't be confused if contracts you've seen use other names. "Provider" stands in for "Licensor," "Transferor," "Vendor," "Seller," and "Consultant," among others. And "Recipient" stands in for "Licensee," "Transferee," "Customer," "Buyer," and "Client." This book favors "Provider" and "Recipient" because they're generic. But the text does occasionally use names like "Distributor" where necessary to avoid confusion.

Fifth and finally, this book includes the world's shortest glossary (at the end). It explains nine terms and phrases you'll see repeatedly in the text: *calendar year, calendar month, calendar quarter, including without limitation, machine-based service, mask works, object code, source code,* and *without limiting the generality of the foregoing.*

PART ONE

Transactional Clauses

The transactional clauses are the key terms in most technology contracts. They provide for the fundamental transaction: the exchange of software or services for money or other consideration.

Most software and services contracts include two of the clauses described in this part: (1) a transfer or sale of software rights or services (Chapters I.A through I.F) and (2) a promise of payment (Chapter I.G). But combination contracts—agreements with multiple transactions—may include several transactional clauses.

A. Standard End User Software License

A license grants the recipient rights to copy software or to exploit it in other ways. It leaves ownership with the provider. A license works like a rental agreement. The provider/landlord still owns the house, but the recipient/tenant gets to use it.[1]

This chapter looks at standard end user licenses: the central clause in an end user license agreement (EULA). In a standard license, the recipient gets the right to run software for internal business purposes. It can't share the software with third parties or modify it.

A software license is a copyright license, but this chapter doesn't go far into the mechanics of copyright. That kind of knowledge isn't usually necessary for a standard license. If you want a deeper understanding of licensing, or if your license doesn't fit the "standard" model discussed here, see Chapter I.C ("Software Licenses in General").

Before drafting your license, ask yourself: *what* is being licensed? The contract should clearly define the "Software" or "Licensed Product"—in the license clause itself, or in a separate definitions section. In a standard license, it's usually enough to give the software's name and version number, and specify object code: "'Software' refers to Provider's *GlitchMaster* software application, version 3.0, in object code format." But if the software has multiple modules or libraries or whatever, or if you see any chance of dispute about what's included, list the necessary elements, and involve someone with technical expertise if necessary. "'Licensed Product' refers to Provider's *RoboSurgeon for the PC* software application, version 2.0, in object code format, including the following modules: RemoteScalpel, Anesthesia-Alarm, and MalpracticeManager." You might also specify the platform: Windows, Macintosh, Linux, etc. Finally, if the

---

1. Software as a service (SaaS) deals are sometimes confused with software license agreements, but the two aren't very similar from a contracting point of view. For SaaS, see Chapter I.F.

recipient needs to reproduce user manuals and other documentation, the definition should include them: "The Licensed Product includes Provider's standard user manuals and other documentation for such software."[2]

1. Reproduction and Use

End user licenses employ various terms for the rights granted. Most license clauses grant rights to "use," "run," "install," "download," "copy," or "reproduce" software. These terms have commonsense meanings, but many of them overlap. This chapter sticks to "reproduce" and "use," to avoid throwing around too many overlapping terms. I recommend you do the same for your end user licenses.

The recipient should always get the right to *use* the software. *Reproduction* rights, on the other hand, aren't always necessary. If the provider delivers ten copies—ten CDs, for instance—and the recipient only needs ten, the license doesn't need the right to reproduce. The same goes for downloaded software. If the recipient can keep downloading copies until it has the correct number, it doesn't need reproduction rights. Of course, technically speaking, you reproduce software every time you install it, but the right to use software implies the right to make a single installed copy. The recipient only needs reproduction rights if it can make more copies than the provider delivers—for instance, if the provider sends one CD or allows one download, and the recipient needs ten copies. In that case, the license should grant the right to *reproduce* and *use* ten copies.[3]

If the recipient can reproduce the software, the license should specify the number of copies, as in the first example in the following clause box. At least, that's the case for most deals. Some contracts call for an "enterprise license." In an enterprise license, like the second example in the clause box, the recipient can make as many copies as it needs. A provider should only grant an enterprise license if it knows the size of the recipient's business and knows it won't expand much—or if the fees are high enough to cover any likely expansion.

---

2. For more on documentation, see Chapter II.C.

3. Actually, the explanation above glosses over some legal complications. If you'd like to know more about copyright license rights, see Subchapter I.C.1—particularly the bullet point on *Use and Other Pseudo Rights*.

Standard End User Reproduction and Use

Provider hereby grants Recipient a nonexclusive license to reproduce and use __ copies of the Licensed Product, provided Recipient complies with the restrictions set forth in this Section __.

• • • •

Provider hereby grants Recipient a nonexclusive license to reproduce and use the Software as necessary for Recipient's internal business purposes, provided Recipient complies with the restrictions set forth in Subsection ___ (*Restrictions on Software Rights*). Such internal business purposes do not include use by any parent, subsidiary, or affiliate of Recipient, or any other third party, and Recipient will not permit any such use.

• • • •

Provider hereby grants Recipient a nonexclusive license to use the Licensed Product, provided: (a) Recipient may give no more than __ concurrent users access to the Licensed Product; and (b) Recipient complies with the other restrictions set forth in this Section __.

• • • •

Provider hereby grants Recipient a nonexclusive license to use the Software, provided Recipient: (a) deploys the Software to no more than __ seats; and (b) complies with the other restrictions set forth in this Section __.

Enterprise license providers should also consider limiting software use to the recipient itself and forbidding use by subsidiaries, parent companies, and other affiliates. Again, see the second example.

Some software sits on a single server computer, and users access and use it from their own "client" computers (desktop, laptop, etc.), without making new copies. If the license for one of these "client-server" systems allows sixty "concurrent users," the recipient may allow sixty users at one time. The software could be physically available to hundreds of users and client computers, but it's restricted to sixty at a time. See the third example in the clause box.

A client-server license might instead allow a fixed number of "seats," as in the fourth example in the clause box. If the license authorizes fifteen seats, it generally means fifteen designated users can access the software, and no others. Jane Employee can't access the software unless she's one of those fifteen, even if fewer than fifteen are accessing the software at any given time. (If Jane's in the in-group, she probably has one of the fifteen user IDs and passwords.) But note that in some cases, "seats" refers to a number of designated client computers, rather than individuals. Then, only those fifteen client computers can access the software.

All four examples in the previous clause box grant license rights "provided" the recipient complies with certain restrictions. Subchapter 2 below addresses those restrictions.[4]

2. End User Restrictions

End user licenses generally limit the recipient's rights in various ways.

Every license should confirm that the recipient receives only the rights specifically granted and that the provider retains ownership of the software. Providers should also consider stating that individual copies of the software are "licensed," not "sold." In other words, the software isn't like a book you've bought, which you can give away or sell. Rather, it's like music you've downloaded, which you're not supposed to pass around. See the first two sentences of the following clause box.[5]

An end user license should also list certain rights *not* granted. Copyright law grants several exclusive rights to copyright owners. Providers should make sure the license doesn't grant any of those except the right to reproduce (along with the right to use, which isn't actually mentioned in the copyright statute). That's why the example in the clause box provides that the recipient can't exercise the other rights of copyright holders. It can't distribute, modify (create derivative works), or publicly display or perform the software. The recipient also can't sublicense its rights to anyone else. Of course, if the

---

4. The "provided" language helps the provider enforce the restrictions. For an explanation of the "provided" language (as opposed to the restrictions themselves), see Subchapter I.C.1.

5. Providers use this "license vs. sale" language to avoid copyright's "first sale doctrine." For an explanation, see footnote 13 on page 17.

Standard End User Restrictions

Copies of the Software created or transferred pursuant to this Agreement are licensed, not sold, and Recipient receives no title to or ownership of any copy or of the Software itself. Furthermore, Recipient receives no rights to the Software other than those specifically granted in this Section __. Without limiting the generality of the foregoing, Recipient will not: (a) modify, create derivative works from, distribute, publicly display, publicly perform, or sublicense the Software; (b) use the Software for service bureau or time-sharing purposes or in any other way allow third parties to exploit the Software; or (c) reverse engineer, decompile, disassemble, or otherwise attempt to derive any of the Software's source code.

clause is silent on restrictions, a court will probably consider the license limited to the rights specifically granted. But why take chances?

The provider should clarify that the recipient gets no time-sharing or service bureau rights, or any other rights to share the software with third parties. *Time-sharing* means sharing an application with customers or other third parties: letting them use the software too. *Service bureau* usage involves another type of sharing: the recipient keeps the software, but it uses it to process third party data, instead of its own data. Either could cost the provider sales.

The provider should also be sure the license forbids reverse engineering and any other attempt to derive source code from the software.

Finally, the provider should be sure the recipient stops reproducing and using the software when the agreement terminates. This book addresses that issue in Subchapter II.T.4 ("Effects of Termination").

B. Standard Distributor Software License

This chapter addresses licenses to distribute software. In these clauses, the provider authorizes a distributor to transfer copyrighted software to third parties—to end user customers. This chapter, therefore, talks about "distributors" rather than "recipients."

Software licenses are copyright licenses. But like Chapter I.A, this chapter doesn't go far into the mechanics of copyright licensing. That kind of knowledge isn't usually necessary for a standard distributor license. But if you want a deeper understanding of licensing, or if your license doesn't fit the "standard" model discussed here, see Chapter I.C ("Software Licenses in General").

Before turning to the terms of a distributor license, ask: *what* is being licensed? The contract should clearly define the "Software" or "Licensed Product"—in the license clause itself or in a separate definitions section. It's usually enough to give the software's name and version number, and specify object code: "'Software' refers to Provider's *CookieCruncher* software application, version 6.02, in object code format." But if the software has multiple modules or libraries or whatever, and you see any chance of dispute about what's included, list the necessary elements—and involve someone with technical experience if needed. "'Licensed Product' refers to Provider's *Pimp-My-Photo* software application, version 4.05, in object code format, including the following modules: Wardrobe Upgrade, Body Maximizer, and VirtualNoseJob." You might also want to specify the platform: Windows, Macintosh, Linux, etc. Finally, if the distributor needs to distribute user manuals or other documentation, the definition should include them: "The Licensed Product includes Provider's standard user guides and other documentation for such software."[6]

1. Distribution

Not surprisingly, a distribution license grants the right to distribute the software—to pass it around.

Distribution rights are often restricted to a geographic territory (e.g., state, region, country, continent). The distributor has no right to distribute outside that area. The territory might also be defined by industry. For instance: "Provider hereby grants Distributor the exclusive right to distribute the Software for use in Semiconductor Fabrication." If you use an industrial territory, be sure to define the industry or segment clearly. For both types of territories, see the first and last examples in the following clause box.

---

6. For more on documentation, see Chapter II.C.

Standard Distribution Rights

Provided Distributor complies with the restrictions set forth in Subsection __ (*Software Restrictions*) below, Provider grants Distributor: (a) an exclusive license to distribute the Licensed Product within _____ (the "Territory"); and (b) a nonexclusive license to reproduce, use, perform, and display the Licensed Product within the Territory, solely as necessary to market it and to provide technical support to customers.

• • • •

Provided Distributor complies with the restrictions set forth in Section __ (*Software Restrictions*), Provider hereby grants Distributor a nonexclusive, worldwide license to exploit the Software as follows, solely as an embedded component of Distributor's Product: (a) to distribute the Software; (b) to reproduce, use, perform, and display the Software for sales and marketing purposes and to the extent necessary to provide technical support to customers of Distributor's Product; and (c) to sublicense to its customers the right to reproduce and use the Software. Distributor may sublicense to its subdistributors the rights granted in Subsections __(a) through __(c) above.

• • • •

Distributor may solicit sales of the Software within _____ (the "Territory"), and Provider will pay Distributor the commission set forth in Section __ (*Payment*) for all Software sales within Territory, whether or not initiated or closed by Distributor. Provided Distributor complies with the restrictions set forth in this Section __, Distributor may use, reproduce, publicly perform, and publicly display the Software to the extent reasonably necessary to market it as authorized in the preceding sentence.

The right to distribute may be exclusive or nonexclusive. If it's exclusive, no one, not even the provider, has authority to distribute within the territory—or anywhere if the license is worldwide. See the first example in the clause box. (Exclusive distribution creates some risks for the provider. See Subchapter 3.)

Some distribution licenses include limited rights to reproduce, use, perform, or display the software, as in all three examples in the previous clause box. These rights help with marketing and technical support. Technically speaking, the clause should grant those rights. But sometimes it's fair to assume a distributor has reasonable marketing and support rights, even if they're not spelled out.

Value-added reseller (VAR) licenses grant limited distribution rights. The distributor can only give the software out as a component of some larger application—often something the distributor itself produces. Imagine the provider makes databases and the distributor makes factory-management applications, which use databases. A VAR license lets the distributor distribute the provider's database *with* the distributor's application, giving end user customers a complete package. But the distributor can't distribute the database as a stand-alone product. The second example in the clause box is a VAR license.

Original equipment manufacturer (OEM) licenses grant the same basic rights as VAR licenses. Technically speaking, in an OEM license, the distributor's product is always equipment—hardware— while a VAR license may involve hardware or software. But to many IT professionals, the terms are interchangeable.

Some distribution licenses let the distributor sublicense its rights to its subdistributors, as in the second example in the clause box. Providers should make sure the contract's payment clause requires royalties or other payments, whether it's a distributor or subdistributor that makes the sale.[7] Some clauses also let the distributor sublicense certain rights to customers. In the second example in the clause box, the distributor can grant its customers the right to reproduce and use the software. Few distribution licenses actually specify these rights, though. Most providers and distributors assume that sublicensing rights are implied in the right to distribute—and that's usually a fair assumption.

Technically speaking, the third example in the clause box is a sales representation clause, rather than a distribution clause. (And the example's first sentence is just a promise, not a copyright license.) The distributor markets the software in the territory but doesn't distribute it. The provider signs contracts with the distributor's custom-

---

7. For more on payment clauses, see Chapter I.G.

ers and distributes the software to them. The example also provides that the distributor is the *exclusive* sales rep in the territory. That doesn't necessarily mean the distributor is the only one marketing the software. The provider can market too, but the distributor gets a commission on every sale in the territory.

All three examples in the clause box grant license rights "provided" the distributor complies with certain restrictions. Subchapter 2 below addresses those restrictions.[8]

2. Distributor Restrictions

License clauses usually restrict distributors in several ways.

The provider should clarify that it still owns the software and that the distributor receives only the rights specifically granted. And usually the provider should forbid reverse engineering and any other attempt to derive source code from the software.

The provider has another party to worry about, besides the distributor. What will the distributor's *customer* do with the software? That's why the license clause should require that the distributor have its customers sign agreements that restrict software use. Often, the provider and distributor draft a full-length end user license agreement (EULA), as in the example in the following clause box. But the parties might instead draft a set of minimum standards for the EULA. "Distributor will not distribute copies of the Software to any third party that does not first execute a written end user license agreement ("EULA") that: (a) forbids distribution of the Software, service bureau or time-sharing use of the Software, or other exploitation Software, except internal use and reproduction to the extent specifically authorized by such EULA; (b) restricts use of the Software to the same extent as, or more than, Subsection 2(a) (*Software Restrictions*); (c) provides for Software audits, with terms no less restrictive than those of Section 9 (*Software Audit*); (d) requires that such third party cease using and delete all copies of the Software after termination of such EULA, and (e) provides that Provider may

---

8. The "provided" language helps the provider enforce the restrictions. For an explanation of the "provided" language (as opposed to the restrictions themselves), see Subchapter I.C.1.

Standard Distributor Restrictions

This Agreement grants Distributor no title to or ownership of the Software, and Distributor receives no rights to the Software other than those specifically granted in this Section __. Without limiting the generality of the foregoing, Distributor will not reverse engineer, decompile, disassemble, or otherwise attempt to derive any of the Software's source code. Distributor may license copies of the Software to its customers but may not sell such copies, and neither Distributor nor its customers will receive title to or ownership of any copy or of the Software itself. Distributor will not distribute copies of the Software to (a) any subdistributor that does not first execute a written contract with limits on Software rights no less restrictive than those set forth in this section__; or (b) any customer or other third party that does not first execute a written end user license agreement in the form attached to this Agreement as Attachment A (*EULA*).

---

enforce the EULA as an intended third party beneficiary."[9] For more on customer (end user) restrictions and contracts, see Subchapter I.A.2.

The clause should also require that the distributor's customers receive *license rights* to their copies of the software, not ownership of those copies. In other words, the software isn't like a book the customer buys, which it can give away or resell. Rather, it's like downloaded music, which the customer isn't supposed to pass around.[10] See the example in the clause box above.

In a sales representation deal, you don't need all the restrictions in the clause box above. The last two sentences—on licensing of copies and customer contracts—aren't necessary because the provider handles all the licensing and contracts directly.

---

9. For software audits, see Chapter II.P ("Software Audits"). For deletion of software after contract termination, see Subchapter II.T.4 ("Effects of Termination"). Finally, an "intended third party beneficiary" is someone who benefits from promises made in a contract and has the right to enforce them, but who isn't a party to the contract.

10. Providers use this "license vs. sale" language to avoid copyright's "first sale doctrine." For an explanation, see footnote 13 on page 17.

Minimum Obligations to Distribute
Distributor will exercise its best efforts to market and sell the Software. Without limiting the generality of the foregoing, if Distributor fails to achieve gross revenues of $_____ from Software distribution during any calendar year, Provider may revoke the license granted in this Section __ by written notice to Distributor.

Finally, the provider should be sure the distributor stops distributing the software when the agreement terminates. This book addresses that issue in Subchapter II.T.4 ("Effects of Termination").

3. Minimum Obligations to Distribute

What if the provider grants an exclusive distribution license and the distributor doesn't bother to market or sell? The software has been "shelved": taken off the market. That's particularly disastrous for the provider if its compensation comes from royalties: from a portion of the distributor's sales. Twenty percent of zero is zero.

The example in the clause box above requires that the distributor *try hard* to sell the software. But "best efforts"—the legal version of "try hard"—isn't very clear. And the best efforts requirement doesn't help the provider if the distributor has a lousy sales team. That's why the clause box also provides that the distributor can lose the license if it fails to hit a certain sales figure. Or as an alternative, the clause could revoke the exclusivity provision, rather than the whole license, if the distributor misses its numbers.

C. Software Licenses in General

Chapter I.A addresses standard end user software licenses, while Chapter I.B addresses standard distribution licenses. This chapter provides a more thorough review of software licensing—of copyright licensing. It provides concepts you can use to customize clauses that don't fit those standard models. But the previous two chapters do explain some key concepts. So before reviewing this chapter, read I.A if you're working on an end user license, and I.B for a distributor license.

This chapter addresses two issues. Subchapter 1 asks: *What license rights does the provider grant?* And Subchapter 2 asks: *What is the scope of the license?* Are the rights exclusive, temporary, restricted, etc.—and if so, how? Software licensing is a game of mix and match. You list the recipient's rights and then match them with the appropriate scope terms.

Subchapter 3 uses all these lessons to show you an "unrestricted license." An unrestricted license grants the recipient as many rights as possible without actually transferring ownership. Recipients who pay for software development sometimes want this sort of license.

Always start by clearly defining the "Software" or "Licensed Product." For guidance on these definitions, see Chapter I.A for end user licenses and I.B for distributor licenses. Also, note that in technology development contracts, it's often impossible to identify all the software at the time the contract's drafted. There, the definition should read something like: "'Licensed Product' refers to all software to be created pursuant to this Agreement." (Unlike the examples in Chapters I.A and I.B, development contracts also sometimes include source code in the definition.)

1. Copyright License Rights

Software licenses are copyright licenses. Under U.S. federal law, the copyright owner has certain exclusive rights. In a license, the owner grants the recipient some of those rights.[11]

The license should list the rights granted. And for the provider's sake, the license should also list the rights that are *not* granted, to make sure there's no confusion. Finally, most licenses should confirm that the recipient receives no *ownership* interest.

Often, the most important terms of a software license are the scope terms, addressed in Subchapter 2. But for now, let's look at rights without scope terms, or with very limited scope terms.

The bullet points on pages 16–18 list the copyright license rights:

---

11. The copyright statute is found at Title 17 of the United States Code (U.S.C.).

Just to muddy the waters, some software is patented, as well as copyrighted. But software recipients generally don't need patent licenses. See Appendix 2 ("Copyrights, Patents, and Other Intellectual Property Rights").

Copyright Licenses (with Limited or No Scope Terms)

Provided Distributor complies with the restrictions set forth below in Subsection __, Provider hereby grants Distributor a license: (a) to modify the Software as authorized in the Specifications; (b) to reproduce the resulting derivative work (the "Derivative Work"); (c) to distribute the Derivative Work; (d) to reproduce, publicly display, and publicly perform the Derivative Work as reasonably necessary for marketing purposes; (e) to sublicense to its customers the right to reproduce the Derivative Work; and (f) to sublicense to its distributors the rights granted in Subsections __(b) through __(e) above. Provider retains full title to and ownership of the Software.

• • • •

Provider grants Recipient a license: (a) to use, publicly display, and publicly perform the Software on the worldwide web; (b) to reproduce the Software to the extent reasonably necessary for such purposes; and (c) to sublicense the rights granted in Subsections __(a) and __(b) to _____ ("Sublicensee"); provided Recipient complies with the restrictions set forth in Subsection __ (*Restriction on Software Use*), and provided Recipient does not modify the Software, distribute the Software to any third party other than Sublicensee, or exercise any copyright holder's rights not specifically granted in this Section __. Copies of the Software created or transferred pursuant to this Agreement are licensed, not sold, and Recipient receives no title to or ownership of any copy or of the Software itself.

• • • •

Provider grants Recipient a license to distribute copies of the Software and to use, publicly perform, and publicly display the Software at any trade show or other marketing venue. Recipient will not modify the Software, sublicense any of the rights granted in this Section __, or reproduce the Software except as strictly necessary for the exercise of the rights granted in the preceding sentence. Provider retains full title to and ownership of the Software.

• • • •

Provider grants Recipient a license to use the Software, provided Recipient complies with the restrictions set forth in this Section __. Recipient may not distribute, modify, publicly perform, or publicly display the Software, and may not reproduce the software except as necessary to install it and to create one backup copy. Copies of the Software created or transferred pursuant to this Agreement are licensed, not sold, and Recipient receives no title to or ownership of any copy or of the Software itself.

- *Reproduce:* The right to make copies. The license clause may authorize one copy, a thousand, or any number, including "such copies as are necessary for Recipient's business operations" (known as an *enterprise license*). See the first three examples in the previous clause box.
- *Modify* or *Create Derivative Works:* The right to change a copyrighted work, creating a new version. See the first three examples in the clause box. (The recipient—or whoever wrote the modifications—owns the new code. But the provider owns part of the derivative work too: the original software.)
- *Distribute:* The right to hand out copies, for payment or for free. This right is necessary for software distributors, including resellers. See the first three examples in the clause box.
- *Publicly Perform:* The right to perform a copyrighted work—to present a movie or play, or to read a novel aloud in a commercial setting. This right has not traditionally applied to software. But software used to run a website *is* arguably performed for the public. The same goes for software demonstrated at a trade show. See the first three examples in the previous clause box.

  For some software, like applications that run websites, public performance rights are probably implied by the right to reproduce or use, even if not specified. If the recipient can't publicly perform software that runs a website, what's the point? Still, if you're the recipient, you're better off including the right, just to be sure.
- *Publicly Display:* The right to show copies to the public. This right has traditionally applied more to visual images than to

software. But software running a website—or demonstrated at a trade show—can often be considered displayed, just as it can be considered performed. See the first three examples in the previous clause box.

As with public performance rights, software public display rights might be implied even if not specified.

- *Use and Other Pseudo Rights:* Some contracts grant the right to "use" software, or "run" it, or words to that effect. See the second, third, and fourth examples in the previous clause box. These terms authorize the recipient to *operate* software. Even a clause granting the right to "install" or "download" authorizes operation, because once you've downloaded or installed software, you don't need separate permission to operate it. I call these "pseudo rights" because they're not listed in the copyright statute, unlike the rights discussed previously. Technically speaking, the pseudo rights aren't necessary. If the recipient already has a copy of the software, or a license to reproduce, it doesn't need an additional grant of rights to use or run the software, because those aren't monopoly rights of copyright holders. (After all, you don't need a license to "use" a copyrighted book: to read it.) Still, there are some legal advantages to including pseudo rights, particularly for providers.[12] And rights to "use" software have become so common that many of your contracting partners will insist on them.

All the pseudo rights imply the right to make one copy of the software. If the recipient can "use" or "install," it has to make a copy for its computer.[13] The problem with pseudo rights is that it's hard to tell what *else* they mean, since we don't have a statute to define them. If the recipient can "install," can it also modify the software, if that's necessary to make the installation effective? Does "use" simply mean the recipient can reproduce one copy and operate it, or does it also include rights to publicly perform and display? The answer will depend on the context—on whether

---

12. By granting the right to "use," "install," or "run," providers bolster their argument that the recipient doesn't *own* its copy of the software. That helps providers avoid copyright's "first sale doctrine," explained in footnote 13 below.

13. In addition to the obvious implication of terms like "use," the copyright statute clarifies reproduce-to-install rights for some recipients. "[I]t is not an infringement for the owner of a copy of a computer program to make . . . another copy . . . provided: (1) that such a new copy . . . is created as an essential step in the utilization of the computer program in conjunction with a machine . . . or (2) that such new copy . . . is for archival purposes only. . . ." 17 U.S.C. § 117(a).

the pseudo right implies other rights, as a result of the software's nature. Because of that uncertainty, both parties should handle pseudo rights with care. If you're the provider, make sure to list the statutory license rights that are *not* granted, as in the fourth example in the clause box on page 16. That way, you confirm that "use" or "install" or whatever does not include any rights you didn't intend. And if you're the recipient, make sure the license specifically grants the *other* rights you need: the statutory rights to reproduce, distribute, etc. "Recipient may use, reproduce, and modify 10 copies of the Software." Don't assume ill-defined pseudo rights will cover all your needs.

- *Sublicense:* The right to pass license rights on to third parties. The license clause could authorize the recipient to take one or more of the rights granted and pass them on to its own customers or distributors or whomever. See the first three examples in the clause box on page 15.

   The right to sublicense is sometimes confused with the right to distribute. Distribution rights allow the recipient to hand out *copies*, not to transfer *rights*. However, sublicensing rights are sometimes implied by distribution rights, when the distributor gives its customers the *right* to reproduce the software. So the two terms can overlap.

Software providers should consider addressing three other issues in their license rights clauses.

First, providers should consider stating that the individual copies of the software are "licensed," not "sold." See the second and fourth examples in the clause box on pages 15–16. In other words, the software isn't like a book someone's bought, which he can give away or sell. Rather, it's like music he's downloaded, which he's not supposed to pass around.[14] Of course, if the provider doesn't care what happens to the authorized copies—so long as the recipient doesn't make new ones—or if the recipient is *supposed* to distribute copies, the language isn't necessary.

---

14. Providers use this "license vs. sale" language to avoid copyright's "first sale doctrine" (17 U.S.C. § 109). The first sale doctrine provides that if you own a copy of a book or painting or photo or other copyrighted work, you can sell that particular copy without infringing copyright. You just can't make new copies. It's not clear how the first sale doctrine applies to software, so the strategy recommended above may not always protect the provider. But until the law gets clearer, it's worth a try.

Second, the provider should be sure the recipient or distributor stops reproducing, distributing, using, and otherwise exploiting the software when the agreement terminates. This book addresses that issue in Subchapter II.T.4 ("Effects of Termination").

Third, providers should consider granting provisional rights, as in the first, second, and fourth examples in the clause box on pages 15–16. The examples grant license rights "provided" the recipient or distributor complies with certain restrictions. The restrictions in question are common license restrictions, like the prohibitions against reverse engineering listed in the clause box, as well as any restrictions included among the scope terms discussed in Subchapter 2. The point of the "provided" language is to help the provider *enforce* those restrictions. The language helps establish that the restrictions are conditions on the license, as opposed to separate contract promises (a.k.a. "covenants"). If the restrictions qualify as license conditions, the recipient (or distributor) loses its license rights if it violates the conditions. The recipient also subjects itself to copyright infringement damages. On the other hand, if the restrictions are separate contract promises, the recipient may not lose its license rights, and it's only liable for standard contract damages, which may be less effective than copyright infringement damages.

Unfortunately, the law hasn't clearly defined the type of restrictions that can be considered license conditions. Obviously, it's in the provider's interest to tie any and all contract provisions to a software license, so it can cancel the license and get copyright damages if the recipient breaches. But I doubt the courts will consider any old restriction a license condition, just because it follows a license clause and the word "provided." Until the law gets clearer, I recommend that you use the "provided" proviso for restrictions closely related to the right to exploit the software. For instance, restrictions on the number of concurrent users who can access software probably qualify as license conditions. The same goes for restrictions on reverse engineering and on distribution outside a given territory. But a clause saying the recipient will make payments by the first of each month probably doesn't qualify. Nor does a promise to keep the provider's business plans confidential. Those restrictions have little to do with exploitation of the software, so I doubt courts will treat them as license restrictions, even if attached to a "provided" proviso.

2. Scope Terms

Scope terms add extra detail to a copyright license, once the copyright holder's rights have been granted. They're limited only by your imagination. Once you've granted rights to the software, you can restrict or define those rights in almost any way, or not at all.

Below are the most typical scope terms:

- *Restrictions on Use, Access, Deployment, etc.:* The provider can limit the recipient to certain uses of the copyrighted work. Software providers often restrict recipients to "internal use." But the license clause can do just the opposite, authorizing "service bureau use"—meaning the recipient can process its customers' data—as in the first example in the clause box below. Providers also limit recipients to a fixed number of seats, concurrent users,

---

Copyright Licenses with Scope Terms

Provider grants Recipient a license to use the Software for "service bureau" processing of third party data and to reproduce the software as necessary to support such use; provided: (a) Recipient will deploy the Software to no more than 30 seats; (b) Recipient will not use the Software to process more than 5,000 Transactions per day; and (c) Recipient will comply with the other restrictions on use of the Software set forth in this Section ___.

• • • •

Provider grants Distributor an exclusive license to distribute the Licensed Product in _____ (the "Territory").

• • • •

Provided Recipient complies with the license restrictions set forth in this Section ___, Provider hereby grants Recipient a perpetual, irrevocable, worldwide, nontransferable, nonexclusive, fully paid, royalty-free license to reproduce, use, and modify the Licensed Software.

or transactions.[15] The first example in the clause box limits both seats and transactions. The following limits concurrent users: "Recipient may reproduce 2 copies of the Software, provided no more than 25 concurrent users may access either copy." If your deal requires restrictions on use, don't hesitate to get creative about drafting them. For instance, the following would be perfectly legitimate: "Recipient agrees not to use the Software on the first Monday of any calendar month, not to install the Software on any computer used to process pet food inventories, and not to permit access to the Software by anyone other than a podiatrist certified to practice in the State of Maryland." (As noted in Subchapter 1 under *Use and Other Pseudo Rights*, some licenses grant permission to "use" software or "install" it or whatever, in the rights clause. The same license might turn around and provide a scope term *restricting* that use or installation.)

- *Exclusivity:* License rights may be exclusive to the recipient. The provider is promising not to grant the same rights to anyone else, or to exercise those rights itself. So in the second example in the previous clause box, the right to distribute in the territory is exclusive to the distributor. Or the license clause might do the opposite. The recipient might receive a "nonexclusive" right to distribute, reproduce, etc., as in the last example in the previous clause box.[16]

As noted in Chapter I.B, an exclusive right to distribute software can blow up in the provider's face if the recipient/distributor has no clear obligation to market the software. See Subchapter I.B.3.

- *Territory:* This scope term restricts license rights to certain areas: usually geographic, but sometimes defined by industry. In the second example in the previous clause box, you'll have a geographic territory if you fill in the blank with "the States of Oregon and Washington." The following defines territory by

---

15. For an explanation of "seats" and "concurrent users," see Subchapter I.A.1.

16. Exclusivity has some consequences. For one, the recipient essentially *owns* the transferred right; it owns a piece of the copyright. So the recipient can sue third parties for infringement of that particular right. In other words, if the recipient has an exclusive right to distribute in Virginia, and someone else distributes in Virginia, the recipient has legal standing to sue that person. (To help enforce their rights, recipients with exclusive licenses should consider registering their licenses with the U.S. Copyright Office.)

industry: "Distributor may distribute the Licensed Product within the Dental Office Equipment Market."

On the other hand, if you want to clarify that there are *no* territorial restrictions, the license should be "worldwide," as in the last example in the clause box. (The term "worldwide" isn't strictly necessary because the law will usually assume a license has no territorial limits, but it never hurts to be clear.)

- *Duration:* Unless the contract provides otherwise, license rights last as long as the term of the agreement. But a license can last longer than the underlying contract, or it can end earlier. The end of a license can be pegged to a calendar date or to a date to be determined. Here is a date to be determined: "The license rights granted in this Section 2 will continue so long as Recipient is a party to a services contract with Provider's subsidiary, Neeto-Service, Inc." Another option is a "perpetual" license, as in the last example in the clause box. With a perpetual license, the underlying contract may terminate—ending the recipient's payment obligations and most other promises—but the license rights last forever, unless they're revoked. (The termination clause should confirm that "perpetual" really means "survives termination," to remove any doubt. See Subchapter II.T.4.)

- *Revocability:* If a license is "irrevocable," the provider can't take it away, even if the recipient breaches the contract. If the recipient doesn't pay, the provider's only remedy is to sue for the money. The provider has given up any right to a court order forcing the recipient to stop using the software. At least, that's the generally understood meaning of "irrevocable." But courts' interpretations vary. Recipients can increase their chances of a broad interpretation by clarifying: "Provider's remedies for breach, including breach of Recipient's payment obligations, may include monetary damages, but Provider hereby waives any right to termination of the license granted in this Section 2."[17] Providers, on the other hand, can protect themselves with terms that delay irrevocability until payment: "The license granted in

---

17. Actually, "irrevocable" licenses can be revoked in one of two ways. First, the copyright statute lets the author (the programmer) revoke a license after thirty-five years, no matter what any contract says. 17 U.S.C. § 203. Usually, no one cares after that long. Second, it's always possible that a court won't honor irrevocability, particularly if the recipient refuses to pay and has no good reason. Courts don't like clauses that seem unfair.

this Section __ will become irrevocable upon Recipient's payment of the License Fee." (An irrevocable license is not necessarily perpetual. The provider can't revoke the rights, but the contract might still specify a natural expiration date.)

- *Payment Scope:* A "royalty-free" license, like the last example in the clause box on page 20, requires no royalty payments. That doesn't necessarily mean the recipient gets the license for free. The contract might call for a fixed payment or for payment under some other scheme (usually appearing in the payment clause, not the license clause). The point is that the recipient doesn't have to pay more every time it makes a copy or otherwise exercises its license rights. If the license is "fully paid"—also like the last example in the clause box—the parties agree that whatever payments are required, if any, have already been made as of the moment the license is granted. If the license is effective "upon Recipient's payment of the License Fee," for instance, and there are no royalties, the license is "fully paid" when granted. (When used together, as in the last example, the two terms provide overlapping protection for recipients.)

- *Transferability:* A license clause can provide that the rights granted are "nontransferable," as in the last example in the clause box on page 20. In other words, the recipient can't give the license to anyone else. Or the clause can say that the license *is* "transferable." Note that sometimes these terms are unnecessary. Most contracts have an assignment clause governing the transfer of rights. If the assignment clause says the contract is or is not transferable ("assignable"), there's no need to repeat it in the license clause.[18] (A transfer is not the same as a sublicense. In a transfer or assignment, the recipient/licensee gives away all its license rights—the whole contract—and is left with none. In a sublicense, the recipient/licensee keeps its rights, but authorizes a third party to exercise them.)

---

18. See Chapter III.I ("Assignment"). Note that there are two kinds of "assignments." Here, we're talking about an assignment of an entire contract, with all its rights and obligations. "Assignment" also refers to a transfer of ownership rights in a copyright or other intellectual property. (For that sort of assignment, see Subchapter I.D.1.)

If the license rights are non-transferable, but the entire contract is assignable, what you have is a mess. The two clauses contradict each other, at least arguably, and it's hard to say which governs.

Scope terms may apply to all the license rights granted or only to some. For instance, the right to reproduce software may be perpetual, while the right to distribute lasts only one year. Or the right to distribute may be exclusive within a particular territory and nonexclusive outside the territory.

Scope terms should appear in the license clause itself. That makes the contract easier to understand. But you may run into contracts with scope terms spread around.[19]

3. Unrestricted License / Deliverables License

An unrestricted license throws in the kitchen sink. The provider grants all the rights of copyright holders, with a broad scope. The license authorizes the recipient to do just about anything with the software, but the provider still owns it and can grant licenses to third parties.

Recipients sometimes want these superbroad licenses when they pay for software development. The recipient is paying the provider to create the software and the project's other "deliverables," so it wants a more or less unlimited right to exploit those deliverables. Of course, the contract could simply give the recipient ownership of the deliverables—of the copyright and possibly other IP rights. But providers often charge more for ownership because it keeps them from selling the deliverables to third parties, on future projects.

The clause box below grants a superbroad license. But it's actually possible to draft a broader one. Some of the rights granted could

---

Unrestricted Copyright License

Provider hereby grants Recipient a nonexclusive, perpetual, irrevocable, worldwide, transferable, fully paid, royalty-free, nonexclusive license: (a) to reproduce, modify, distribute, publicly perform, publicly display, and use the Licensed Software; and (b) to sublicense any or all such rights to third parties.

---

19. Recipients should consider one other scope-like provision: a bankruptcy rights clause. See Chapter III.M.

be exclusive. If *all* the rights were exclusive, however, the seller would have no copyright left. The transaction would work like an assignment—a transfer of copyright ownership to the recipient—despite the word "license."[20]

The example in the clause box doesn't include the "provided" language discussed in Subchapter 1: the language saying the license is conditional on the recipient's compliance with the contract's various restrictions. Many providers granting superbroad licenses don't care about ensuring copyright remedies (which is what's at stake in these "provided" provisos). But if the provider does care, it should add the language.

D. Software Ownership: Assignment and Work-for-Hire

An ownership clause provides that the recipient will *own* software, including intellectual property rights in software. An ownership clause may give the recipient other assets too, like user manuals or logos.

This chapter explains the key types of ownership transfers: work product clauses and transfers of existing assets. But first, this chapter addresses the legal vehicles used in all ownership clauses: assignments and work-for-hire provisions.

Before executing an ownership contract, the recipient should ask itself why it wants to *own* the software. In software development agreements, the recipient often argues: "We paid to have it made, so we own it." But if the recipient only plans to *use* the application—if it doesn't sell software—it may get little value from ownership. A license could provide all the rights the recipient needs, particularly if it's an "unrestricted license," like the one in Subchapter I.C.3. And the provider might charge less for a license because if it retains ownership, it can generate additional revenue by granting licenses to third parties.[21]

---

20. See Chapter I.D.

21. Licenses do have a disadvantage. A license is a contract right, and contracts can be terminated. An assignment gives an ownership right, which is harder to terminate, and the same goes for a work-for-hire clause, which is essentially nonterminable. (See the following explanation of work-for-hire.) In general, however, if your license agreement is well crafted, termination shouldn't be a major concern.

Ownership clauses are complicated, and a lot can go wrong, particularly for the recipient. As noted previously, you should always consider experienced legal help when drafting IT contracts, but all the more so for the clauses explained in this chapter.[22]

• • • •

An assignment clause transfers ownership from the provider to the recipient. "Provider hereby assigns to Recipient all its right, title, and interest in and to the Software and Documentation."[23] Usually, IT assignments transfer *all* the provider's rights: copyrights, patents, other forms of intellectual property, and anything else—and that's the case with the assignments discussed in this book.[24]

A work-for-hire clause, on the other hand, doesn't transfer ownership because the provider isn't the owner and never was. Under a work-for-hire clause, the recipient owns the software from the moment it's written, even though *the provider* writes it. In other words, work-for-hire reverses the law's usual assumption—that the author of a writing owns it.

Work-for-hire applies to copyright only, not to patents or other forms of IP. Many work-for-hire contracts, however, *also* include assignment clauses that transfer patent and other rights—and that's the case with the clauses discussed on page 27.

You can't create a work-for-hire relationship just by writing it into a contract. Work-for-hire status applies to two fact patterns. In the first, the provider is the recipient's employee and writes the software or other assets within the scope of his or her employment. In the second fact pattern, the software or other assets fit into one of copyright law's nine "eligible" categories, listed in the following, and the parties agree in writing on work-for-hire status.

The first fact pattern is simple, so long as there can be no doubt about the provider's employment status. If the provider is an em-

---

22. The recipient should also consider registering any copyrights acquired, and filing patents and trademarks where appropriate. The U.S. Library of Congress handles copyright registration, while the Patent and Trademark Office handles patents and trademarks (obviously). Again, consider experienced legal help.

23. For documentation, see Chapter II.C.

24. Note that there are two kinds of "assignments." Here, we're talking about a transfer of ownership rights in a copyright or other intellectual property. "Assignment" also refers to the transfer of an entire contract, with all its rights and obligations. (For that sort of assignment, see Chapter III.I.)

For the differences between copyrights and patents, see Appendix 2

ployee, and his or her job involves the software programming in question—or the documentation creation or whatever—the deal passes the test. In fact, a written contract isn't entirely necessary, since generally the law will consider the employment a work-for-hire relationship. But for the recipient/employer, it's better to avoid doubt by including a work-for-hire clause in the employment contract, or if that agreement isn't in writing, by signing a software ownership contract. Also, the employee might create assets that aren't subject to work-for-hire treatment—patentable inventions, for instance—and a written contract would address them too. See Subchapter 1.

It's often hard to tell whether a relationship qualifies as "employment." What if the provider serves part-time or works from home with no health benefits? Unfortunately, the law doesn't provide a clear test. Courts consider a long list of factors in determining employment status. So if you want to use work-for-hire and you're not absolutely sure the provider is an employee, consider some experienced legal help. You should also consider backing up your work-for-hire clause with an assignment, as explained in Subchapter 1.

The second fact pattern allows work-for-hire treatment through a written contract, even if the provider isn't an employee working in the scope of his or her employment. "The Software and Documentation will be considered works made for hire pursuant to the U.S. Copyright Act, 17 U.S.C. Section 101 *et seq.*, and will be Recipient's sole property." But that clause only works if the deal fits one of the copyright law's nine eligible categories. The recipient has to order the software "as a contribution to a collective work, as a part of a motion picture or other audiovisual work, as a translation, as a supplementary work, as a compilation, as an instructional text, as a test, as answer material for a test, or as an atlas."[25] Legal scholars debate the extent to which software can fit into these nine categories. One thing is clear: the nine categories are complicated, so if in doubt, seek experienced legal help. And again, consider backing up your work-for-hire clause with an assignment, as explained in Subchapter 1.

For recipients, work-for-hire clauses are better than assignments because they can't be revoked. Revocation of assignments is rare, but it's possible in some situations. (In fact, all copyright assignments and licenses can be revoked after thirty-five years, no matter what

---

25. 17 U.S.C. § 101

the contract says.[26]) But of course, work-for-hire treatment isn't always available.

1. Ownership of Work Product

This subchapter addresses ownership of "work product": software or other assets created through professional services relationships, research and development agreements, and similar collaborations. In most cases, the work product doesn't yet exist when the parties execute the contract.

If you're the recipient, you should consider a work product clause when you engage a software programmer (either an individual or a company), assuming you want to own the software created through the relationship. But technology creation isn't restricted to programmers. Almost any tech-savvy service provider could create IT assets. For instance, a phone support contractor might write a set of instructions for handling tech support calls—or even come up with an improvement to the recipient's product. So recipients should consider work product clauses in all their services contracts. They should also consider them in their employment contracts.

The example in the following clause box assumes the provider is an independent contractor and an individual, rather than a company—a freelance software programmer, for instance. But the clause works just as well if the provider is the recipient's employee—though you might then switch "Provider" to "Employee" and "Recipient" to "Employer" or "Company."[27] Also, the clause works just as well if the provider is a company, providing service through its employees. In that case, however, the example's invention reporting and prior invention provisions—Subsections (a) and (d)—might not make sense. A substantial company might not be willing or able to report all its prior or current inventions. Also, if the provider is a company, the recipient should consider a clause requiring that the provider's employees sign a work product ownership contract too.

---

26. See 17 U.S.C. § 203

27. Recipients should be aware that some state laws restrict employers' rights to require assignments of inventions. California, for instance, restricts the types of inventions the employer can demand, and requires that the employer notify the employee of that legal restriction. (Cal. Labor Code §§ 2870-2872.) If in doubt about your state, get experienced legal help

Ownership of Work Product

(a) *Reporting of Inventions.* Provider will promptly disclose to Recipient all computer software programs, other works of authorship, formulas, processes, compositions of matter, databases, mask works, improvements, logos, symbols, designs, and other inventions that Provider makes, conceives, reduces to practice, or creates, either alone or jointly with others, during the period of the Provider's engagement with Recipient (collectively, "Inventions"), whether or not in the course of such engagement, and whether or not such Inventions are patentable, copyrightable, protectable as trade secrets, or otherwise subject to intellectual property protection.

(b) *Recipient Ownership of Work Product.* An Invention will be considered "Work Product" and will be Recipient's sole property if it fits any of the following three criteria: (1) it is developed using equipment, supplies, facilities, or trade secrets of Recipient; (2) it results from Provider's work for Recipient; or (3) it relates to Recipient's business or its current or anticipated research and development.

    (i) Work-for-Hire. To the extent permissible under applicable law, Work Product will be considered work made for hire pursuant to the U.S. Copyright Act, 17 U.S.C. § 101 *et seq.*, and any foreign equivalent thereof.

    (ii) Assignment. To the extent, if any, that Work Product may not be considered work made for hire, Provider hereby assigns to Recipient all of its ownership, right, title, and interest in and to all Work Product, including, without limitation: (A) all copyrights, patents, rights in mask works, trademarks, trade secrets, and other intellectual property rights and all other rights that may hereafter be vested relating to the Work Product, arising under U.S. or any other law, together with all national, foreign, state, provincial, and common law registrations, applications for registration, and renewals and extensions thereof; (B) all goodwill associated with Work Product; and (C) all benefits, privileges, causes of action, and remedies relating to any of the foregoing, whether before or hereafter accrued (including without limitation the exclusive rights to apply for such registrations, renewals, and/or extensions, to sue for all past infringements or violations of any of the foregoing, and to settle and retain proceeds from any such actions).

(c) *Backup License.* To the extent, if any, that this Section ___ does not provide Recipient with full ownership, right, title, and interest in and to the Work Product, Provider hereby grants Recipient a perpetual, irrevocable, fully paid, royalty-free, worldwide license to reproduce, create derivative works from, distribute, publicly display, publicly perform, use, make, have made, offer for sale, sell or otherwise dispose of, and import the Work Product, with the right to sublicense each and every such right.

(d) *Prior Inventions.* Provider represents that Exhibit A attached to this Agreement is a list of all Provider's Inventions prior to the Effective Date which Provider has not separately assigned to Recipient (collectively "Prior Inventions"), and that if Exhibit A is blank or not included, there are no Prior Inventions. Provider will not use any Prior Invention in Provider's work related to the engagement with Recipient without Recipient's prior written consent. To the extent that Provider does use or incorporate a Prior Invention in a product, service, or process created for Recipient, with or without Recipient's consent, Provider hereby grants Recipient a non-exclusive, perpetual, irrevocable, fully paid, royalty-free, worldwide license to reproduce, create derivative works from, distribute, publicly display, publicly perform, make, have made, offer for sale, sell or otherwise dispose of, import, and use such Prior Invention, solely in conjunction with the product, service, or process in question, with the right to sublicense each and every such right.

(e) *Moral Rights.* In addition to the foregoing transfers and allocations of rights, Provider hereby irrevocably transfers and assigns to Recipient any and all "moral rights" Provider may have in or with respect to the Work Product. Provider also hereby forever waives and agrees that it will never, even after termination of its engagement with Recipient, assert any of the following against Recipient or its customers, licensees, or sublicensees (direct and indirect): (i) any moral rights with respect to the Work Product; and (ii) any moral rights with respect to the Prior Inventions licensed pursuant to Subsection __(d) above. "Moral rights" include any rights to claim authorship of or credit on a work of authorship, to object to or prevent the modification or destruction of a work of authorship, or to withdraw from circulation or control the publication or distribution of a work of authorship, and any similar right, existing under judicial or statutory law of any country or subdivision of a country, or under any treaty, regardless of whether or not such right is described as a "moral right."

(f) *Further Assistance.* Provider will help Recipient obtain and enforce patents, copyrights, rights in mask works, trade secret rights, and other legal protections for the Work Product in any and all jurisdictions throughout the world. Provider will execute any documents Recipient reasonably requests for use in obtaining or enforcing such rights and protections. To the extent that such assistance occurs after Provider's engagement with Recipient, Recipient will compensate Provider at a reasonable rate for time and expenses spent at Recipient's request pursuant to this Subsection __(f). Provider hereby appoints Recipient or its designated representative as Provider's attorney-in-fact to execute documents on Provider's behalf for the purposes set forth in this Subsection __(f).

(g) *Survival.* The rights and obligations of this Section __ will survive any termination or expiration of this Agreement or of Provider's engagement with Recipient.

See Subsection (e) in the clause box in Subchapter 2 (page 36), as well as the explanation in the text following that clause box.

The recipient's first concern is reporting. It can't claim ownership of software or other assets if it doesn't know about them. So Subsection (a) in the clause box (page 29) requires that the provider report all software and inventions created during the engagement, even if they're not related to the engagement.

Next, the clause determines which inventions are "work product": software and other assets owned by the recipient. Subsection (b)'s definition includes any software or other asset related to the recipient's business, even if it's created after hours, and any asset created with the recipient's computers or other facilities, even if it has nothing to do with the recipient's business. That's a common definition, but it's also pretty favorable to the recipient. The provider might try to narrow it. For instance: " 'Work Product' refers to any Invention conceived, developed, or reduced to practice during the course of Provider's work for Recipient." Or, to narrow the definition even further: " 'Work Product' refers to any software related to the Pest Management Industry created during the course of Provider's work for Recipient." (That assumes the contract has clearly defined the "Pest Management Industry.")

The previous clause box includes both a work-for-hire clause and an assignment, in Subsections (b)(i) and (b)(ii). Work-for-hire only relates to copyright, so the assignment helps the provider claim patentable inventions and other IP rights. The assignment is also backup for the work-for-hire terms. If the latter can't be enforced, everything is assigned. Whatever happens, the recipient should own all the work product.

For a cautious recipient, even that sort of overlapping protection leaves too much risk. That's because some jurisdictions, particularly certain foreign ones, bend over backwards to protect creators from their own contracts and don't reliably enforce assignments. So a good assignment clause includes a royalty-free backup license, as in Subsection (c) (page 30). The license grants the recipient full rights to exploit the software, even if it doesn't get full ownership.

The backup license in Subsection (c) grants rights under both copyright and patent law. Most software licenses address copyright only, because that's almost always enough. But the license in the previous clause box isn't a traditional software license. It's a stand-in for *ownership* of software and other assets. It's meant to come as close to ownership rights as possible. That's why it addresses patent holders' exclusive rights: the rights to use (or exclude others from using), make, have made, offer for sale, sell or otherwise dispose of, and import products incorporating the invention.[28]

Sometimes, courts and government agencies won't honor an assignment unless the provider signs special forms or cooperates in other ways. It's hard to know in advance what kind of cooperation you'll need. So Subsection (d) in the clause box (page 30) requires whatever reasonable cooperation the recipient may eventually request. Subsection (d) also provides that the recipient will be the provider's "attorney-in-fact." In other words, if the provider is unavailable to sign IP ownership or enforcement documents in the future, the recipient can sign them as the provider's representative.

Subsection (e) in the clause box addresses a similar concern. Some foreign countries give authors "moral rights" over their work. (The United States does too, but to a very limited extent.) Moral rights vary, but often they include rights to be identified as the author and rights to prevent mutilation or revision of the work. The recipient rarely wants the provider to retain that kind of control, so Subsection (e) waives moral rights. Recipients should be warned, however, that in many foreign countries, moral rights *can't* be waived or fully waived.

Finally, Subsection (f) asks the provider to list all his or her prior inventions. Work product assignments cover new work only, and often the provider couldn't assign prior inventions even if he or she wanted to, because third parties own them. So recipients want to identify prior inventions in advance, to head off disputes, and they want those inventions kept out of the work product. Subsection (f) goes a step further. If the provider includes a prior invention in the work product anyway, despite all these precautions, the provider grants the recipient a broad license to exploit it (like the backup license in Subsection (c)). Providers, of course, should hesitate before granting such a license, particularly if third parties own some or all of their prior inventions. Of course, providers can protect themselves by keeping prior inventions out of their work product.

---

28. For more on patents and the difference between them and copyrights, see Appendix 2. (Also note that *both* patent and copyright licenses typically address the right to "use" software.)

2. Transfer of Existing Assets

This subchapter addresses software and other assets the provider created on its own and wants to give to the recipient, rather than "work product" created specifically for the recipient.

As with licenses, the contract should clearly define the "Software," "Assigned Materials," or whatever you're calling the assets in question. If there's any chance of dispute about the content of those assets, make sure to list all modules, libraries, bug fixes, documentation, etc. Generally, a definition for software assets should specify all forms of code: object code, source code, etc. It might also include any documentation necessary to understand the software. For instance: "The 'Assigned Materials' refers to Provider's *DuckTracker* software application, including without limitation: (1) all versions thereof; (2) object code, source code, machine code, and all other forms of software code; and (3) all user manuals and related technical documentation Provider has at any time published or distributed to customers, or included in internal development and quality assurance manuals, for use with the *DuckTracker* software."

The example in the following clause box includes an assignment, a backup license, a moral rights clause, and a further assistance clause—just like the work product ownership language discussed in Subchapter 1. So for explanations of those terms, see Subchapter 1.

In other words, the two clauses are similar. But the following clause lacks a work-for-hire provision. That's because work-for-hire doesn't fit a transfer of *existing* assets. Work-for-hire addresses assets created specifically for the recipient, but here the provider created the software separately, before executing the contract. That distinction lies behind all the differences between the two clauses.

What if the provider has employees or contractors who helped write the software? Did each contributor execute a valid contract, giving the provider full rights it can then transfer to the recipient? If not, those contributors will own part of the software. If the recipient has any doubt about employee or contractor rights, it should have them sign separate contracts, as required by Subsection (e) (page 36). The form for these separate assignment contracts would be an attachment to the main agreement, and its central clause

Transfer of Existing Assets

(a) *Assignment.* Provider hereby assigns to Recipient all of its ownership, right, title, and interest in and to the Software, including, without limitation: (i) all copyrights, patents, rights in mask works, trademarks, trade secrets, and other intellectual property rights, and all other rights that may hereafter be vested relating to the Software, arising under U.S. or any other law, together with all national, foreign, state, provincial, and common law registrations, applications for registration, and renewals and extensions thereof; (ii) all goodwill associated with the Software; and (iii) all benefits, privileges, causes of action, and remedies relating to any of the foregoing, whether before or hereafter accrued (including, without limitation, the exclusive rights to apply for such registrations, renewals, and/or extensions, to sue for all past infringements or violations of any of the foregoing, and to settle and retain proceeds from any such actions).

(b) *Backup License.* To the extent, if any, that this Section __ does not provide Recipient with full ownership, right, title, and interest in and to the Software, Provider hereby grants Recipient a perpetual, irrevocable, fully paid, royalty-free, worldwide license to reproduce, create derivative works from, distribute, publicly display, publicly perform, use, make, have made, offer for sale, sell or otherwise dispose of, and import the Software, with the right to sublicense each and every such right.

(c) *Moral Rights.* In addition to the foregoing transfers and allocations of rights, Provider hereby irrevocably transfers and assigns to Recipient any and all "moral rights" Provider may have in or with respect to the Software. Provider also hereby forever waives and agrees never to assert any moral rights with respect to the Software. "Moral rights" include any rights to claim authorship of or credit on a work of authorship, to object to or prevent the modification or destruction of a work of authorship, or to withdraw from circulation or control the publication or distribution of a work of authorship, and any similar right, existing under judicial or statutory law of any country or subdivision of a country, or under any treaty, regardless of whether or not such right is described as a "moral right."

(d) *Further Assistance.* Provider will help Recipient obtain and enforce patents, copyrights, rights in mask works, trade secret rights, and other legal protections for the Software in any and all jurisdictions throughout the world. Provider will execute any documents Recipient reasonably requests for use in obtaining or enforcing such rights and protections. Recipient will compensate Provider at a reasonable rate for time and expenses spent at Recipient's request pursuant to this Subsection __(d). Provider hereby appoints Recipient or its designated representative as Provider's attorney-in-fact to execute documents on Provider's behalf for the purposes set forth in this Subsection __(d).

(e) *Employees.* Provider will require that all its employees and contractors in any way involved in creating the Software execute assignment agreements with Recipient in the form attached hereto as Exhibit A. Provider will reasonably cooperate with Recipient in assuring such employees' and contractors' compliance with the terms of Exhibit A.

(f) *Survival.* The rights and obligations of this Section __ will survive any termination or expiration of this Agreement.

would be identical to Subsections (a) through (d) and Subsection (f) of the clause box. (But replace "Provider" with something like "Assignor" or "Staff-Member.")[29]

---

29. Note that Subsection (e) in the clause box gives the recipient a contract right against the provider, not against the employees (or independent contractors). If the employees never actually sign their separate assignment contracts, the recipient can sue the provider for breach of contract, but it may not be able to get any ownership rights from the employees. (Also, see footnote 27 on page 28 for restrictions on employers' rights to require assignments from employees.)

E. Programming, Maintenance, Consulting, and Other Professional Services

In a services contract, the provider agrees to help the recipient. This chapter addresses *professional* services.

This book distinguishes professional services from machine-based services. The two overlap, but in general, professional services rely on people. A human being is the service provider, though he or she may use a computer. Professional services include tech support, computer programming, software maintenance, website design, and IT consulting. Machine-based services, on the other hand, rely almost entirely on computers. For instance, you might call your Internet service provider and talk to a human (if you can get through), but the human doesn't provide the real service. A computer connects you to the Internet, so Internet connectivity is a machine-based service. So are web hosting, most online security systems, and "software as a service" offerings. Chapter I.F addresses machine-based services.

A professional service clause says, essentially: "Provider will provide the following services to Recipient: _____." This chapter addresses the blank: the terms defining the service. This chapter also addresses midstream changes in the service, terms for multiple distinct services (multiple statements of work), and terms covering service provider qualifications.

Obviously, professional services clauses appear in contracts addressing programming, IT consulting, and other human-based services. But they also crop up in many software contracts. In a software license agreement, for instance, the provider often provides maintenance or tech support, in addition to software. And in a software development agreement, the provider develops software—a service—and licenses or sells it to the recipient.

1. Defining the Service

Services descriptions can be task-driven or outcome-driven. Task-driven descriptions favor the provider. In provisions like the first two examples in the following clause box, all the provider has to do is perform the tasks listed. "Provider will provide two employees to

Description of Services

During Business Hours, Provider will staff the Help Desk with no fewer than 2 technicians. Through such technicians, Provider will exercise its best efforts to resolve computer and user errors promptly, in response to Recipient technical support requests.

•   •   •   •

Throughout the term of this Agreement, Provider will: (a) make 3 Consultants available to Recipient during Business Hours to assist with system integration; and (b) produce a system development report 30 or more days after the end of each calendar quarter, providing detailed descriptions of system development progress.

•   •   •   •

Provider will write an employee benefits software application that conforms to the technical specifications set forth in Exhibit A (the "Software"). Provider is not required to provide support or maintenance for the Software except to the extent provided in Section ___ (*Warranty*).

•   •   •   •

For a period of _____ following the Implementation (as defined below) of the System, Provider will maintain the System so that it performs according to the Specifications during no less than 98% of each calendar month ("Maintenance"). Thereafter, Maintenance will renew every _____, unless Recipient notifies Provider of its intent not to renew ___ or more days before any renewal date. After Maintenance has renewed _____ times, Provider may refuse any subsequent renewal by written notice _____ days before the next renewal date. ("Implementation" refers to the date Provider certifies to Recipient in writing that installation and customization are complete and that the System is ready for use in production.)

do the following . . ." The recipient might be unhappy with the outcome, but that's not the provider's problem (at least, legally).

Outcome-driven descriptions, like the last two examples in the clause box, favor the recipient. "Provider will achieve the following outcomes . . ." The provider can't point to a list of tasks and say: "I tried." If the provider doesn't achieve the outcome, it hasn't met its obligations.

Clarity is particularly important in services descriptions, and particularly difficult. On fixed price deals, providers often suffer from "scope creep": the job gets bigger but the price doesn't. A clear description of the services helps prevent scope creep, because the provider can say: "Look, that's not included in the contract; it'll cost extra."

Recipients should protect themselves from unclear descriptions too. They should make sure the contract promises all the expected help. Is technical support required? How about bug fixes? After-hours support? Is special equipment required, and if so, who supplies it?

Both parties should be sure to keep the recipient's tasks out of the services description. Don't draft a description like the following: "Provider will provide the following services: (1) Recipient's project manager will meet with Provider by June 17 and outline the specifications, and Provider will then prepare the first specifications draft . . ." That makes no sense because the provider can't make the recipient show up at that meeting. To avoid confusion, list the recipient's tasks separately, in their own attachment or clause. With the recipient's tasks elsewhere, the previous provision might read: "Within 10 business days of the first specifications meeting with Recipient, Provider will deliver the first specifications draft."

Finally, Providers and recipients sometimes argue over *when* the services start. In a software agreement, does maintenance start on the day the provider delivers the software or on the day the system goes into service? How about tech support? If the provider will be customizing the software or needs time for installation, recipients should consider starting support after those tasks are done. In some deals, support does no good until then, so why pay for it? The provider is already working on the system, and the recipient probably isn't using it, so payment for maintenance or tech support would be payment for nothing. That's why the last example in the previous clause box starts support on the date of *implementation*. If you use a clause like that, make sure to define "Implementation" in a way that fits your deal. You might, for instance, define it as "acceptance of the final Deliverable pursuant to the [implementation] Statement of Work," or "the date on which customization and installation are complete and the System materially performs according to its Technical Specifications."[30]

Providers, on the other hand, generally prefer to start support on delivery, so that support *fees* start as early as possible. "Starting on delivery of the System, Provider will provide the maintenance services described in Attachment B for the monthly fees set forth in Section 6." Providers often have good reasons to start early—even during the implementation process. They sometimes make certain staff and other resources available through the maintenance process, and customization and installation might be difficult without those resources. Plus, many maintenance clauses include the right to updates and upgrades.[31] If maintenance doesn't start until after implementation, the recipient could miss out on improvements to the software. Also, for some providers, maintenance fees "upon delivery" are built into the price of the software and related services. Maybe the recipient really *doesn't* need maintenance until after customization and installation, but license fees and related service fees would be higher if maintenance fees started later.

2. Change Orders and Midstream Terminations

Often, the recipient wants to change the services partway through the project, or wants to terminate them. This subchapter addresses both change orders and midstream termination.

Change orders let the parties modify the services without a new contract. See both examples in the following clause box. You don't really need a change order; you could just amend the contract to add new services. But a change-order procedure is easier. For the provider,

---

30. See Chapters II.F ("Delivery, Acceptance, and Rejection") and II.A ("Technical Specifications").

Some recipients go even further. They call for a support start date at the end of the warranty period. In many cases, a warranty of function is essentially a temporary free maintenance clause, so recipients might not need maintenance during the warranty period. But that logic doesn't always work. Maintenance often involves support that's not provided through the warranty clause. See Subchapter II.J.1 ("Warranty of Function").

31. See Chapter II.D ("Updates and Upgrades").

Change Order Clauses

The parties may agree to additional or modified services through a written change order, and such change order will become part of this Agreement when executed by both parties.

• • • •

Recipient may request that Provider add features to the Software not in the Technical Specifications by submitting a written change order to Provider, in the form attached hereto as Exhibit B. Provider will negotiate in good faith regarding price and other terms related to such additional features, and any change order will become part of this Agreement when executed by both parties.

---

it offers an easy way to add new revenues to a project. And for the recipient, clauses like the second example above require that the provider offer relatively reasonable prices and terms for the new work. ("Good faith" isn't the clearest of contractual obligations, but it's better than nothing for the recipient, and sometimes it's the best the parties can agree on in advance.)

If you do create a change-order procedure, consider a change-order *form*, as in the second example in the clause box. That way, a casual exchange of letters or e-mails won't count as a change order. The form could read: "Pursuant to the March 13, 2006, Technology Services Agreement between Obsequio, Inc. ('Provider') and Scope-Creep LLC ('Recipient'), Provider will provide the additional services listed below, and Recipient will pay the additional fees listed below . . ." Or, you could create a more elaborate form. If you'd like a more elaborate model, see the statement of work form in the second clause box in Subchapter 3. If you use that model, replace "Statement of Work" with "Change Order" throughout the form.[32]

What if, instead of changing the project, the recipient kills it, by failing to cooperate? For instance, the provider might need to meet

---

32. Change orders usually apply to changes in project scope, while statements of work apply to whole new projects. But beyond that difference, the two are similar. So if change orders play a major role in your contract, review Subchapter 3 on multiple statements of work.

Midstream Termination

Recipient's failure to provide the staff required by the Statement of Work for any Recipient task or joint task, within __ business days of Provider's written request, will constitute termination of this Agreement pursuant to Subsection __ (*Termination for Convenience*).

• • • •

Recipient's failure to make the Facility available to Provider's personnel for more than __ business days out of any calendar month will constitute a material breach of this Agreement.

---

with the recipient's chief technology officer to provide the services. What if the recipient doesn't make the CTO available, or fires him or her? If the provider did a good job drafting the services description, that will count as breach of contract. But it's hard to anticipate every risk in a services description. So providers should consider a backup clause addressing midstream termination.

Midstream termination clauses protect providers by closing the "noncooperation" loophole. The recipient's failure to cooperate might count as termination for convenience, which often requires early termination fees, as Subchapter II.T.3 explains. See the first example in the clause box above. Failure to cooperate might also count as breach of contract, as in the second example in the clause box.

3. Multiple Statements of Work

Often, the parties plan on several projects over a long period, and they can't identify all the work when they draft the contract. Some recipients and providers handle this by negotiating an amendment to the contract for each new project. That's messy and confusing. A better solution is the multiple statements of work format. The contract acts as an umbrella—a master services agreement—and it doesn't have to be amended. When the parties agree on a new project, they fill out a new statement of work.

The body of the contract should set up the statement of work procedure, as in the example in the following clause box. It's usually

---

Multiple Statement of Work Procedure

Provider will provide such services as are required by any statement of work in the form attached hereto as Attachment A, executed by each party ("Statement of Work"). Upon execution, a Statement of Work will become part of this Agreement. In the event of any conflict with a Statement of Work, the terms of this main body of this Agreement will govern.

---

best to include a statement of work *form* to fill out, again as in the example. (See the clause box on the next page for statement of work forms.) That's better than letting the parties use any old Word document, e-mail, notepad, or napkin. Use of a form helps keep careless employees from agreeing to new projects without realizing it, and without proper review. Some clauses go further and provide: "No statement of work will become part of this Agreement or bind either party unless signed by each party's Project Manager" (or some other officer).

What if a statement of work contradicts the main body of the contract? What if the statement says the provider owns all IP rights in the work product, but the contract says the recipient does? Conflicts like that should be rare, because statements of work should stick to project details and avoid issues already addressed in the contract. But mistakes happen. The best remedy is a clause providing that, in case of conflict, the contract overrules the statement of work, as in the example in the clause box above. That protects your hard-won contract from careless revision through the statement of work process. If the parties really want to change the contract, they can explicitly amend it. Usually, an amendment involves more review, so you can make sure no one is giving away the farm.

Some companies, however, want maximum flexibility in their statement of work process, and they let the statement of work trump the contract. I think that's a bad idea. But if you insist, make sure to limit the reach of the statements of work, in the contract's main body: "The terms of a Statement of Work will govern in the event of a conflict with the terms of this Agreement, but only with respect to the work set forth in such Statement of Work and not with respect

Statement of Work Form

STATEMENT OF WORK NUMBER ____
To Technology Services Agreement

Project Title: _____

This Statement of Work Number __ (this "Statement of Work") is entered into pursuant to the _____ Technology Services Agreement (the "Agreement") by and between _____ ("Provider") and _____ ("Recipient").

This Statement of Work is incorporated into the Agreement. In the event of any conflict between this Statement of Work and the main body of the Agreement, the main body will govern. The provisions of this Statement of Work govern only the subject matter hereof and not any other subject matter covered by the Agreement. Capitalized terms not otherwise defined in this Statement of Work will have the meanings given in the main body of the Agreement.

I. *Services & Deliverables.* Provider will provide the following services: _____
[Insert description of services. Include technical specifications for any technology to be created, or include reference to specifications attached to this Statement of Work.]

II. *Recipient Cooperation.* Recipient will reasonably cooperate with Provider in the provision of services and will provide the following assistance to Provider: _____
_____ *[Insert description of Recipient responsibilities, or insert "N/A" if not applicable.]*

III. *Payment.* Recipient will pay Provider as follows: _____
_____ *[Insert payment schedule. Insert any payment/invoicing terms not already covered in main body of Agreement. If none of the preceding applies, insert: "Client will pay for Services pursuant to the requirements of Section __ of the Agreement."]*

IV. *Additional Provisions.* In addition, the parties agree as follows: _____
[Insert additional terms or "N/A" if not applicable.]

> This Statement of Work is effective as of the latest date of execution set forth below.
>
> ***signature block for both parties***

to any other work to be performed pursuant to this Agreement, including without limitation pursuant to any other Statement of Work."[33]

The statement of work form should give the parties enough flexibility to craft a project. It should also require that each new statement of work get a number, to enable project tracking. And the form, once complete, should be signed by both parties.

In the clause box statement of work form above, the italicized text in brackets is part of the form. It provides instructions for future statement of work drafters. You never need to remove it; just add the necessary text beneath it.

4. Experience and Qualifications

In many professional services deals, the recipient should make sure the provider assigns qualified people—assuming the provider isn't an individual providing services without employees. This concern applies most strongly to task-driven services.

Avoid vague qualifications like "adequate experience." No one knows what that means. Terms like "industry standard experience"

Qualifications
All Provider's employees or contractors staffing the Help Desk will have no fewer than __ years' full-time work experience operating or maintaining _____ and will be certified by a _____ authorized trainer for maintenance of _____.

---

33. For more on conflicts between contract attachments, see Chapter III.N.

work a bit better, if the industry really has a recognized standard. But the best option is to specify concrete qualifications. In the previous clause box, fill in the blanks with the name of the specific system to be maintained or the names of respected training institutions and certification programs.

F. Software as a Service and Other Machine-Based Services

A machine-based service is a technical service provided through computers and software. These include telecommunications and Internet connectivity. They also include systems typically called "software as a service" (SaaS). In SaaS, the provider makes a software application available to the recipient, but the recipient doesn't get a copy. The software sits on the provider's computers, and the recipient accesses it via the Internet or some other communications system.[34]

Machine-based services and professional services overlap, but in general, the latter rely on people more than machines. Professional services include technology consulting and software programming. This book addresses them in Chapter I.E.

The promise of machine-based services is a simple clause. The contract names the service—"Internet connectivity," for example, or "use of Provider's online customer relationship management system"—and the provider promises to make it available.

Where possible, recipients should include a detailed description of the services, as suggested in the third example in the following clause box. But many providers offer machine-based services through standard contracts, with little or no chance to negotiate or add descriptions. Providers should consider services descriptions too. A description can list the tasks the system *won't* perform, and that protects the provider.

This book doesn't provide an example of a services description. But Chapter II.A covers technical specifications while Chapter II.B covers service level agreements—and both will help you describe machine-based services.

---

34. SaaS systems are also known as "application service provider," or "ASP," systems. SalesForce.com is a well-known example of SaaS.

Promise of Machine-Based Services

Provider will provide Recipient with Internet connectivity services, pursuant to Provider's policies listed on the policies page
of Provider's website, as such policies may be updated from time
to time.

• • • •

Provider will give Recipient access to Provider's online financial
management system (the "System"). Provider retains all right,
title, and interest in and to the System, including without limitation all software used to provide the System and all logos and
trademarks reproduced through the System, and this Agreement does not grant Recipient any intellectual property rights
in or to the System or any of its components.

• • • •

Provider will provide information technology security services
that perform according to the technical specifications listed in
Attachment A.

IT professionals sometimes imagine that a software as a service
contract should look like a software license agreement. That's a mistake. In a license agreement, the recipient needs a grant of IP rights—
the license clause—since it's going to make a copy of the software or
take other actions the law reserves to copyright holders.[35] In a SaaS
contract, the recipient never gets a copy of the software, so it doesn't
need a license. License agreements also frequently include rights to
maintenance and to updates and upgrades.[36] In a SaaS deal, the
recipient doesn't need any of those, since the provider maintains,
updates, and upgrades the software on its own computers. Don't be
fooled by the fact that both types of deals address "software." Think
through the differences and draft accordingly. (For a full SaaS form
contract, see this book's website: www.TechContractsHandbook.com.)

---

35. See Subchapter I.C.1 ("Copyright License Rights").
36. See Chapters I.E ("Programming, Maintenance, Consulting, and Other Professional Services"); II.D ("Updates and Upgrades").

Finally, if your deal involves a standardized contract, like on-line terms of service, you should review Appendix 4 ("Clickwraps, Browsewraps, and Other Contracts Executed without Ink"). And if your machine-based service is online, review Appendix 5 ("Online Policy Documents").

G. Payment

In the payment clause, the recipient (or distributor) promises to pay the provider.

The payment clause should specify the goods or services triggering the obligation, particularly if the contract has more than one deliverable. The parties might eventually need to know what's been paid for and what hasn't. Also, a specific payment obligation can help the recipient if the provider goes bankrupt. A bankrupt provider might stop providing services, but the recipient's license rights could remain. If the recipient pays for licenses and services in a lump sum, it might have to keep paying the whole amount to keep its license rights. With separate payments, the recipient could stop paying for the services it's no longer getting and continue paying license fees.[37]

1. End Users' Fees

Many licenses call for a simple one-time payment, as in the first, third, and fifth examples in the following clause box. Others require a stream of payments, as in the second example (and presumably the license terminates if the recipient stops paying). The payment could be called a "license fee," "royalty," or almost anything else. The choice of terms isn't important, so long as it's clear the payment is for software rights.

A thorny issue crops up in development agreements where payment is required when the work is done. What does "done" mean? If the provider says the job's finished but the software doesn't do what the recipient hoped, is it done? The best way to address this is through an acceptance procedure, as suggested by the third and fifth examples in the clause box. (The fourth example may call for acceptance too, because each of the milestones listed could be acceptance of a deliverable.) See Chapter II.F ("Delivery, Acceptance, and Rejection").

---

37. See Chapter III.M ("Bankruptcy Rights").

End User Payments

Recipient will pay Provider $_____ for its rights to the Licensed Product, subject to invoice upon delivery thereof.

• • • •

Recipient will pay Provider a license royalty of $_____ per _____ (the "License Term"), due 30 days before the start of each License Term.

• • • •

Upon Acceptance, Provider may invoice Recipient for the License Fee.

• • • •

Recipient will pay Provider the following amounts, each due 30 days after the following milestones listed in Attachment B (*Development Schedule*):

- Milestone 1: $_____.

- Milestone 2: $_____.

- Final Milestone: $_____.

• • • •

Recipient will pay Provider: (a) $_____ in license fees, due within 30 days of Acceptance (as defined in Section __); and (b) $_____ per calendar quarter for the Services, due on the last day of the preceding calendar quarter.

• • • •

Recipient will pay for Services on a time and materials basis, according to the rate schedule in Exhibit B. Provider will invoice all amounts due on the last day of each calendar quarter. Payment against all invoices will be due within _____ days of receipt thereof.

Service fees can be paid all at once or on a continuing basis, just like license fees. For continuing fees, see the fifth example in the clause box. Terms like "license fee" and "royalty" don't apply to services fees.

Professional services are often billed on a time and materials basis. The recipient pays for the providers' employees' billable hours and for equipment and other materials. Sometimes the materials part of the charge is a simple reimbursement, but sometimes it includes a markup, so the provider can make a profit on the materials. Time and materials payments can lead to disputes. What if the provider spends two hundred hours solving a problem the recipient thinks should take twenty? A good solution is a clause providing something like: "Fees will not exceed $12,000 for any given calendar month unless Recipient agrees in writing in advance." That doesn't mean the provider works for free once it hits the dollar cap. At that point, it can stop and request instructions.

2. *Distributors' Fees*

Distributors typically pay a portion of sales revenues—often called a "royalty"—or a fixed fee per unit.

Royalty obligations can lead to disputes because the amounts due can't be defined in advance. The solution is detail. Providers should make sure the distributor has to report all sales in detail and on a regular basis, as in the first example in the following clause box. Usually, that's the only way to learn how much is due.[38] And, if the provider gets a percentage of revenues rather than a fixed payment, both parties should think through the meaning of "revenues." The provider gets 20 percent of *what*? The example in the clause box gives the provider a percentage of "gross revenues." That's usually relatively simple, but think about whether the parties might dispute the definition. And if the provider gets a percentage of *net* revenues, you definitely need a definition. Decide whether your figure includes sales taxes, commissions, cost of delivery, etc., and wrap those decisions into a definition. For instance: "'Net Revenues' refers to all revenues received from third parties for rights to the Software, in-

---

38. Software audits give the provider additional security. See Chapter II.P.

Distributors' Fees

Distributor will pay Provider a royalty of __ % of gross revenues collected for licenses to the Software; provided such royalty will not fall below $__ per copy distributed, regardless of the revenues collected by Distributor, including without limitation if Distributor collects no revenues. On the _____ business day of each calendar quarter, Distributor will report all Software sales for the preceding calendar quarter, including customer names, units sold, and amounts receivable and received, as well as such additional detail as Provider reasonably requests. Distributor will pay all amounts due within 30 days of such report.

• • • •

Distributor will pay Provider $__ per unit shipped to Distributor, and Provider may invoice Distributor at any time after shipment.

---

cluding revenues from maintenance, minus: (a) sales tax, use tax, and value-added taxes; (b) return credits; and (c) salespeople's commissions."

Providers paid through a percentage of revenues should also consider a minimum royalty. Again, see the first example in the clause box. Without a minimum, the distributor could sell for nothing or next to nothing—as a promotion, for instance—and the provider would get no royalties.[39]

3. Due Dates and Invoices

In some of the last two subchapters' examples, payment is triggered by an event, like delivery or acceptance. The event could also be the effective date, or "30 days after the Effective Date." In other examples above, an invoice triggers payment.

---

39. The solution proposed above fixes a minimum *royalty* paid to the provider, not a minimum *price* for end users. "Vertical price fixing" violates some states' antitrust laws.

Invoices

Provider will submit itemized invoices to Recipient for the payments required by this Section __, and all invoices will be due and payable within 30 days.

•   •   •   •

Invoices serve as confirmation of amounts owed, and Recipient's payments are due on the dates required pursuant to this Section __, regardless of the date of Provider's invoice.

PART TWO

General Clauses

"General Clauses" is a catch-all category, referring to everything that's not a transactional clause or a supporting clause (boilerplate). The following terms account for most of the ink spread across most software and services contracts. The one characteristic shared by all these clauses is that they generate a lot of disagreement, debate, and compromise.

A. Technical Specifications

Technical specifications describe software and computer systems in detail. They say what the technology will do—how it's supposed to perform. In many contracts, they are the most important terms: the *only* ones that will matter in many disputes. Yet businesspeople and lawyers usually pay them little attention.

Technical specifications ("specs") are appropriate for most software contracts, including licenses, assignments, and distribution agreements. They're also appropriate for any professional services contract that involves the creation or maintenance of software or computer systems. Finally, specs are appropriate for many contracts covering software as a service and other machine-based services.[1] In these agreements, the specs describe the service itself: speed of transmission between offices, interface between systems, etc.

Some IT professionals distinguish *functional specifications* and technical specifications. The line between the two isn't clear, but in general, functional specs describe software from the user's point of view: how the screen shots should appear, how the computer will respond to a command, etc. Technical specs are more technical, looking at issues like system architecture and programming languages. This book makes no such distinction. It addresses both under the "technical specifications" heading.

Technical specifications and service level agreements (SLAs) overlap. An SLA is a set of specifications for a machine-based service. But SLAs usually cover other topics too, like repair of malfunctioning services and credits for downtime. This book covers SLA specs here and the other SLA provisions in Chapter II.B.

• • • •

---

1. For professional services and machine-based services, see Chapters I.E and I.F.

The specs provide information used in *other* contract clauses. For instance, here's a warranty clause using technical specifications: "Provider warrants that, during the first 1 year after the Effective Date, the Software will perform according to its technical specifications listed in Attachment A." And here's a maintenance services clause: "Provider will maintain the System so that it performs materially in accordance with its Specifications." Or a development services clause: "Provider will design a software application that conforms to the technical specifications attached hereto as Exhibit B." Or a machine-based services clause: "The Service will perform according to its Specifications during 99 percent of each calendar month." Finally, here's an acceptance clause: "In the event that the software fails the acceptance tests, Recipient will provide a written description of each deviation from the specifications listed in Attachment A, and Provider will repair the software so that it performs in accordance with all its specifications."[2]

1. The Importance of Specifications

Because specs are so technical, many recipients and providers pay them little attention or leave them out. That's a bad choice.

Imagine you're the recipient and you license a widget-tracking computer system for your factory floor. You quickly discover that the system takes too long to generate reports. Worse, it won't sync with your floor managers' handheld computers. You complain to the provider, but you signed a contract with no technical specs. All the contract says is that you bought "WidgetTracker Server Edition 5.02, a computer system for tracking and managing widgets on a factory floor." That doesn't address speed or synchronization. Maybe the provider's salespeople told you the system was fast and could sync, but those promises didn't find their way into the contract, so they don't do you much good.[3]

Now imagine you're the provider. You have a customer who thinks you were dishonest, and you have a dispute on your hands.

---

2. For more on these five clauses, see Subchapters II.J.1 ("Warranty of Function") and I.E.1 ("Defining the Service") and Chapters I.F ("Machine-Based Services") and II.F ("Delivery, Acceptance, and Rejection"), as well as Chapter II.B ("Service Level Agreements").

3. Most contracts have an "entire agreement" or "integration" clause, which is meant to void promises made before the contract was signed. See Chapter III.R.

Ideally, you would point to the contract and say: "Look, the contract says what the system does; it's not required to do anything else." But you can't because the contract has no specs. As the provider, you need specs to clarify what the system will *not* do.

In other words, as this book's introduction explains, good fences make good neighbors. Detailed specifications are excellent fences.

There *are* contracts that don't need detailed specifications. If there's little chance reasonable minds could differ about what the system is supposed to do, specs aren't necessary. For instance, if the deal involves standard off-the-shelf software, with widely known functions, you can often leave out the details. Or you might just provide: "the System will perform according to its technical specifications published by Provider." That assumes, of course, that the provider has published something.

But if in doubt, assume you need specs.

2. Responsibility for Specifications

Who should draft specifications? Recipient or provider? Lawyer, businessperson, or IT staffer?

As between recipient and provider, there is no standard answer. Whoever understands the system best will usually write the first draft. Often that's the provider. But sometimes a recipient drafts specs for an RFP (request for proposal) regarding customized technology, and those specs become part of the ultimate contract.

Both recipients and providers often leave specs drafting to programmers and engineers. That's usually appropriate, but if the businesspeople and lawyers responsible for the deal don't get involved, the specs may not reflect the business's goals. Let's take a contract for a customized human resources computer system. The recipient's technical folks might draft the specs because they're familiar with the technology. But it's the HR staff members who know best what the system should do. If they're not involved, the specs won't fully address HR's needs—and neither will the system.

In other words, whoever is responsible for the deal should play a role in drafting the specs, even if that's a technically challenged businessperson or lawyer.

That doesn't mean a businessperson or lawyer has to write specs from scratch. But if a nontech businessperson or lawyer is responsible for the deal, he or she should go over the specs with the technical staff, to make sure they describe the desired system. And he or she should edit the specs for clarity. If the technically challenged business manager or lawyer can understand the specs, they *must* be clear.

3. Organizing and Editing Specifications

The job of drafting technical specifications lies outside the scope of this book, but this subchapter will help you organize and edit your specs.

There is no standard length. Specs should run as long as necessary to express the business goal for the technology. Nor is there a

---

Technical Specifications Form

ATTACHMENT A: TECHNICAL SPECIFICATIONS

The System will provide the functionality listed below.

Module A: _____. *[Insert name of module. Insert each function below.]*

• Function #1: _____.

• Function #2: _____.

• Function #3: _____.

Module B: _____. *[Insert name of module. Insert each function below.]*

• Function #1: _____.

• Function #2: _____.

• Function #3: _____.

Module C: _____. *[Insert name of module. Insert each function below.]*

• Function #1: _____.

• Function #2: _____.

• Function #3: _____.

standard organization. Specs might appear as a narrative: an essay describing machine-based services or software. But unless the specs are very short, numbered clauses usually work better. The specs could appear as a list of numbered bullet points, for instance, or as an outline.

The previous clause box is a blank form: one of many options for organizing technical specifications.

The language should be clear and simple. For instance, Function #1 of Module A might read: "Module A will process employment applications and create an Excel spreadsheet for each, in the format described below under 'Reports.'" That's a very functional description. But even if the specs are more technical, the language should remain clear.

Edit specifications the same way you'd edit any contract clause. Make sure each concept gets a simple and clear description. Limit technical jargon. And when the specs must use a technical term, provide a clear definition.

4. Specifications as a Deliverable

In some technology services projects, the provider is required to write technical specifications as a contract deliverable. So detailed specs aren't available in advance, at the time the contract's drafted. But the parties must have *some* vision of the technology—some idea what the provider is supposed to create. That vision should be written into the contract, as high-level specs, with more detail to follow, as a deliverable.

If your deliverables include specifications, you should create a system for accepting them. At some point, the parties should agree in writing that *these* are the specs. "Provider will deliver detailed specifications for the System within 90 days of the Effective Date. Such detailed specifications will conform to the requirements set forth in the High-Level Specifications attached to this Agreement as Exhibit B, and if they do not so conform, Recipient may reject them by providing written notice to Provider within 10 days of delivery." Acceptance of specs works a lot like software acceptance. For more on acceptance in general—including procedures for redelivery after rejection—see Chapter II.F.

B. Service Level Agreements

"Service level agreement" refers to a clause or set of clauses addressing the performance of machine-based services.[4]

Despite the name, a service level agreement (SLA) is not generally a separate contract. It could be a separate document incorporated into the contract—maybe something attached or posted at a website. Or it could be another set of terms in the contract's main body: "Section 10 - Service Level Agreement."

SLAs tell the recipient any or all of the following: (1) how the service will perform, (2) how the provider will fix the service if it doesn't perform, (3) what kind of credit the recipient gets if the service doesn't perform and/or the provider doesn't fix it, and (4) in rare cases, what kind of extra "incentive fees" the provider gets if the service performs better than required.

The previous point 1—how the service will perform—is the technical specifications for the service. This book addresses technical specifications in Chapter II.A. This chapter covers points 2 through 4.

1. SLA Remedies

There is no required length or format for an SLA. Just express the parties' expectations regarding service remedies.

The key remedy is often repair. The provider promises to fix a faulty service within some set period, as in the first example in the clause box on the following page.

Many SLAs also include credits. See the second example in the clause box. If the service doesn't work, or if the provider doesn't fix it fast enough, the recipient gets a credit—or in some rare cases a refund.

The credit or refund will generally be the recipient's only compensation. The recipient can't get a court to order additional payments as damages for breach.[5]

---

4. See Chapter I.F for machine-based services.

5. That's because SLA credits and refunds are generally seen as "liquidated damages," and liquidated damages are usually exclusive remedies. See Chapter II.Q.

SLA Remedy Terms

Provider will address System faults as follows:

- *Level 1 Error:*   Response within __ minutes; Remedy within __ hours.

- *Level 2 Error:*   Response within __ minutes; Remedy within __ hours.

- *Level 3 Error:*   Response within __ hours; Remedy within __ business days.

As used above:

(a) "Remedy" refers to a solution that returns the System to full performance as required in the Technical Specifications.

(b) "Response" refers to an e-mail, telephone, or in-person acknowledgement of a technical support request.

(c) "Error" refers to any failure of the System to perform as required in the Technical Specifications.

    (i) "Level 1 Error" refers to _____.

    (ii) "Level 2 Error" refers to any failure not constituting a Level 1 or Level 3 Error.

    (iii) "Level 3 Error" refers to _____.

• • • •

Provider will exercise its best efforts to maintain the average round-trip transmission time ("Latency") required in the specifications above (the "Specifications Target").

(a) *Credits.* In the event that average Latency exceeds the Specifications Target during any calendar month, Provider will credit Recipient __ % of such month's applicable service fees for each millisecond above the Specifications Target; provided such credit will not exceed __ % of any month's otherwise applicable service fees. The credits set forth in the

> preceding sentence are Recipient's sole remedy for Latency in excess of the Specifications Target.
>
> (b) *Incentive Fees.* In the event that average Latency falls below the Specifications Target during any calendar month, Provider may invoice Recipient for incentive fees equal to __ % of that month's applicable services fee for each millisecond below the Specifications Target, up to __ % of the applicable service fees.

An incentive works in the opposite direction. If the service performs better than promised, the recipient has to pay extra fees, as in Subsection (b) of the second example above. Incentive fees are appropriate in some cases, but the recipient should ask itself whether better-than-expected performance is worth extra money.

2. Refunds after Termination

What happens to SLA credits if the contract expires, or if someone terminates?

SLAs generally limit the provider's obligations to credits, rather than refunds, and provide that credits disappear if the agreement terminates. See the first example in the clause box below. For the

---

Credits after Termination

Credits issued pursuant to this SLA apply to outstanding or future invoices only and are forfeited upon termination of this Agreement. Provider is not required to issue refunds or to make payments against such credits under any circumstances, including without limitation termination of this Agreement.

• • • •

Provider will issue refunds against any outstanding credits issued pursuant to this SLA within ____ days of termination of this Agreement for any reason.

provider, that policy preserves revenues and gives customers an incentive to stick around.

Some contracts, however, do allow conversion from credits to refunds. See the second example in the clause box. Providers should consider limiting the types of termination that trigger refunds. For instance, the SLA might allow conversion for any termination "other than termination for Recipient's breach."

3. The Material Breach Issue

Many SLAs are silent on a key issue: at what point is service so bad that the recipient can terminate the contract? In other words, at what point do service level errors count as material breach of contract?

Providers generally don't want their customers terminating. But failure to address material breach in the SLA doesn't necessarily protect the provider. At some point, bad service will probably authorize the recipient to terminate, even if the contract says nothing on the issue. By addressing material breach in the SLA, providers can make termination more predictable.

The example in the clause box below authorizes termination for material breach if service falls below a certain level. It also protects the provider by setting a time limit on termination. The recipient can't terminate the contract in July because of bad service in January.

SLA Material Breach and Termination

In the event of ___ or more Level 2 or worse Errors during any calendar month, Recipient may terminate this Agreement for material breach pursuant to the provisions of Section ___ (*Termination*), provided Recipient notifies Provider in writing of termination within ___ days of the end of such calendar month.

C. Documentation

Proper use of software often requires documentation. These documents range from user manuals to design descriptions for programmers and system managers.[6] If documentation is necessary, a software agreement should require that the provider deliver it.

Some software contracts define the "Licensed Product" to include "such software's standard user manual." With a definition like that, the license and delivery clauses will usually give the recipient all the necessary rights. But some contracts address documentation separately.

The first example in the clause box below addresses standard software, with little or no customization. The second addresses software customized for the recipient.

Documentation is written text, just like software, so if the recipient needs to make copies, it should get a license to reproduce or otherwise exploit the documentation. See the second example in the clause box.

Documentation requirements vary widely, so you will likely have to customize a clause to fit your deal.

Documentation

Upon delivery of the Software, Provider will also deliver ____ copies of the Software's standard user manual.

• • • •

Provider will provide such documentation as is reasonably necessary to operate the Customized Software ("Documentation"). Provider will deliver the Documentation to Recipient upon delivery of the Software and will revise the Documentation as reasonably necessary in the event of changes to the Software, without further charge. Recipient may reproduce any such Documentation as reasonably necessary to support internal use of the Customized Software.

---

6. Another type of documentation usually appears *within* source code, so it's not addressed here. This highly technical "code documentation" explains the software's intended operation. If the recipient gets source code, it should automatically get any embedded documentation.

D. Updates and Upgrades

Software licenses sometimes grant the recipient rights to new versions. These "updates and upgrades" range from bug fixes and other minor tweaks to whole new releases. The contract will generally state that updates and upgrades become part of the licensed product—the "Software" or whatever—so the parties don't need to sign a new contract.

Many providers link updates and upgrades to the maintenance clause. The recipient gets new versions if it's paying for maintenance. (Maintenance is a professional service, addressed in Chapter I.E.)

Often the provider wants to distinguish between minor upgrades and major new releases. If the recipient has rights to *Super-Soft* v. 3.00, it should get a free copy of v. 3.04, which corrects bugs

---

Updates and Upgrades

During the term of maintenance pursuant to Section __ (*Maintenance Services*) of this Agreement, Provider will provide Recipient with copies of all new versions, updates, and upgrades of the Software (collectively, "Upgrades"), without additional charge, promptly after commercial release. Upon delivery to Recipient, Upgrades will become part of the Software and will be subject to the provisions of Section __ above (*License*) and the other provisions of this Agreement.

• • • •

Provider will deliver all Minor Upgrades (as defined below) to Recipient promptly after release, and such Minor Upgrades will then become part of the Licensed Product. Recipient may acquire copies of Major Releases (as defined below) at a __ % discount off Provider's standard retail price, and such Major Release will become part of the Licensed Product upon Provider's receipt of payment. "Major Release" refers to any new version of the Licensed Product Provider releases commercially (at its sole discretion) with a new version number to the left of the version decimal point. "Minor Upgrade" refers to any other new version of the Licensed Product.

and makes minor improvements. But *SuperSoft* v. 4.00 has all-new features and may even cost more. So provisions like the second example in the previous clause box require that the recipient pay for these "major releases," though sometimes at a discount.

E. Schedule and Milestones

Some services need a schedule or end date. For example, at some point in a technology development project, the computer system has to be designed, built, and ready for use. Those deadlines appear in a scheduling clause.

The simplest way to handle scheduling is to provide a deadline for completion of the project, as in the first example in the following clause box. But for a long or complex project, you often need several deadlines, or milestones. See the second example. Often, one of the milestones is "Acceptance" or submission to "Acceptance Testing." Those terms are usually defined in an acceptance clause. See the next chapter (Chapter II.F).

Milestones can serve as powerful incentives if they're linked to the recipient's payment obligations, as in the second example. The provider will perform much more quickly if it gets paid at each important step—an obvious benefit for the recipient. And for the provider, a milestones payment structure may be the only way to get some of the fee before finishing the job.

A source of dispute hangs over all scheduling clauses. What if the provider needs the recipient's cooperation to finish on time, and the recipient doesn't cooperate? What if the provider needs instructions from the recipient, or equipment, or access to the building—and the recipient takes forever? The provider shouldn't be held responsible for the delay. Sometimes you can handle this issue through a lockstep scheduling clause: "Recipient will provide an instructions memo within 60 days of the Effective Date. Provider will complete Phase 1 within 30 days of receiving the instructions memo." (See also Subsection 1.C of the second example in the following clause box.) That way, the clock doesn't start ticking on the provider's performance until after the recipient cooperates.

But often the recipient's task is not easily defined. Often the provider needs general and miscellaneous cooperation: a million small favors that will make the project run smoothly. This is one of the

> ### Schedule of Services
>
> Provider will complete the Project on or before _____.
>
> • • • •
>
> 1. *Milestones.* Provider will complete the Service by the following deadlines ("Milestones"):
>
>   A. Alpha Version functioning according to Specifications ("Operational"): _____ after Effective Date;
>
>   B. Beta Version Operational: _____ after Effective Date;
>
>   C. Full System Operational and submitted for Acceptance Testing: _____ after Beta Version Operational.
>
> 2. *Payment.* Recipient will pay Provider in the following installments:
>
>   • Milestone A: __ % of the Development Fee
>
>   • Milestone B: __ % of the Development Fee
>
>   • Milestone C: __ % of the Development Fee
>
>   • Acceptance: __ % of the Development Fee

hardest problems to address in a contract. One solution is to provide extra time to complete each milestone, so that if the recipient fails to cooperate, the provider can still get done on time. Another is to include something like: "All deadlines are subject to such extension as is reasonably necessary if Recipient does not cooperate in good faith with Provider, including by providing the following forms of assistance: . . ." The problem, of course, is that terms like "cooperate," "good faith," and "reasonably necessary" are vague. Try to draft the scheduling clause as clearly as possible, but recognize that you may have to accept some of these wiggle words.

At some point, the recipient's failure to cooperate crosses over into breach or termination of contract. For that issue, see Subchapter I.E.2 ("Change Orders and Midstream Terminations").

F. Delivery, Acceptance, and Rejection

Delivery, acceptance, and rejection clauses are appropriate for most software agreements. At their simplest, they provide instructions for the provider about the time and place of delivery. But some clauses go further and call for "acceptance tests." The recipient can test the software to make sure it works. If the software fails, the recipient can reject it, and the provider usually has to fix it or refund the money.

The first example in the following clause box is a simple delivery provision. The second is an acceptance clause. Acceptance clauses and acceptance testing are most common for customized software: systems the provider creates or modifies to fit the recipient's needs.

The provider should not give the recipient freedom to reject goods for any old reason, or because they don't meet expectations the recipient never mentioned. The clearest test provides that the goods fail if they don't conform to their technical specifications, as in the second example in the clause box.[7] But some contracts lay out much narrower tests, defining steps the recipient can take to test the goods. "The Software will be considered accepted if it passes all three Tests listed on Attachment B."

One risk for the provider is that the recipient will never get around to testing the goods, or will take a long time. That's particularly troubling if the provider doesn't get *paid* until acceptance. That's why many acceptance clauses have a "deemed acceptance" provision, as in the second example in the clause box. If the recipient doesn't either accept or reject within X days, the goods are *deemed* accepted.

What if the goods fail the test? The contract might require that the provider fix them or refund the recipient's money, as in the second example in the clause box.

If the provider tries to fix the goods and redelivers them, the parties could find themselves going around the same rejection, fix, and redelivery loop indefinitely. So an important issue is: who decides when to give up and recognize that the goods won't work? In the second example, either party can give up and go home after the second rejection.

---

7. See Chapter II.A ("Technical Specifications").

Delivery, Acceptance, and Rejection

Provider will deliver one copy of the Software, in compact disk format, to Recipient's facility at _____ within _____ days of the Effective Date.

• • • •

Provider will install the System in Recipient's facility located at _____ on or before _____ days after the Effective Date ("Delivery"). The System will be considered accepted ("Acceptance") (a) when Recipient provides Provider written notice of acceptance or (b) ___ days after Delivery, if Recipient has not first provided Provider with written notice of rejection. Recipient may reject the System only in the event that it materially deviates from the Technical Specifications. In the event of such rejection, Provider will correct the deviation and redeliver the System within ___ days. Redelivery pursuant to the previous sentence will constitute another Delivery, and the parties will again follow the acceptance procedures set forth in this Section ___, except that after any subsequent failure of the System to perform according to the Technical Specifications, either party may terminate this Agreement by written notice (up until such time as the parties agree to continue the acceptance procedures of this Section ___). In the event of such termination, Provider will promptly refund all amounts paid pursuant to this Agreement, as Recipient's exclusive remedy, and Recipient will promptly return all copies of the System.

Some contracts add another remedy for goods that don't pass the test on time: late fees. The provider usually pays late fees through a credit or partial refund: "In the event of Rejection, Provider will credit Recipient 1% of the License Fee for every business day until the delivery date of Software that passes the Acceptance Tests." If you use late fees, review Chapter II.Q ("Liquidated Damages").

Finally, the contract should state whether the recipient's remedies for failure of acceptance tests—and for any related delay—are exclusive. Providers, of course, prefer terms saying the recipient's remedies *are* exclusive, as in the second example of the clause box. In other words, once the provider has fixed the goods or refunded the money, it's off the hook: it isn't liable for breach of contract. Recipients, on the other hand, generally prefer language saying the contract remedies are not exclusive: "The refunds and other remedies set forth in this Section 4 are not exclusive of any other remedies Recipient may have." In that case, recipients should specify that termination of the agreement, in response to rejection, is termination for breach by the provider. (Credits may be unenforceable if they're not the exclusive remedy. Again, see Chapter II.Q.)

G. Technology Escrow

Software recipients often receive object code but not source code. In many cases, the result is that the recipient won't be able to maintain or improve the software, since the technicians need source code to see how the system is supposed to work. That's not a problem if the provider offers any necessary service. But what if the provider goes out of business? Or what if the provider breaches its service obligations? If the system's vital, the recipient will be in trouble. That's why software licenses often include technology escrow provisions.

Technology escrows can cover assets other than source code, but we'll focus on source code because it's common to the transactions addressed in this book.

In an escrow clause, the provider gives a reliable third party a copy of its source code, and of any supporting documentation. This third party, the "escrow agent," holds the materials for the recipient's benefit. The recipient gets the source code if an agreed "release condition" happens. Release conditions usually include the provider's bankruptcy or breach of its service obligations.

The escrow agent is necessary because the recipient can't assume it will get the source code from the provider, if and when the time comes. If the provider someday breaches its service obligations, it might also breach any promise to turn over source code. And if the provider goes bankrupt, the law will relieve it of most contract obligations, like promises to turn over source code.

The escrow agent could be almost anyone the parties trust, but the most reliable services come from companies that specialize in

> ## *Separate Escrow Agreement*
>
> (a) *Escrow Agreement.* Concurrent with execution of this Agreement, the parties will execute a third party escrow agreement in the form attached hereto as Attachment __ ("the Escrow Agreement"), in conjunction with _____ (the "Escrow Agent").

technology escrow.[8] These professional escrow agents generally have their own form contract setting up the relationship. The "escrow agreement" becomes an attachment to the parties' license agreement. Recipient, provider, and escrow agent all sign it—usually at the same time as the recipient and provider sign the license agreement.

Most terms of the separate escrow agreement relate to the mechanics of the parties' relationship with the escrow agent: storage of materials, payment of the agent,[9] etc. Those terms generally appear in a standard form contract from the escrow agent, and this book doesn't address them. This book does address terms governing the relationship between the recipient and provider. Those terms can appear in either the escrow agreement or the main license agreement. If they appear in the escrow agreement, they're usually subject to negotiation and revision by the provider and recipient, unlike the other terms of the escrow agreement.

1. Deposit and Verification

The recipient should make sure the provider gives the escrow agent the right source code and supporting materials.

First and foremost, the escrow clause should list the deposit material, particularly source code and documentation, as in the following Subsection (b). And if the contract doesn't call for documentation, or the documentation isn't very complete, recipients

---

8. Some businesses ask one of the parties' lawyers to serve as escrow agent. That's a bad idea because it creates a conflict of interest. A lawyer should be loyal to his or her client, while an escrow agent should be neutral.

9. Often it's the recipient who pays the escrow agent because the recipient benefits from making the source code available. But the parties may split the fees, and there's no reason the provider can't pay.

Escrow Deposit and Verification

(b) *Deposit.* Within ___ business days of the Effective Date, Provider will deposit with the Escrow Agent, pursuant to the procedures of the Escrow Agreement, the source code for the Software, as well as the Documentation and names and contact information for each programmer involved in creation of the Software. Promptly after release of any update, upgrade, patch, bug fix, enhancement, new version, or other revision to the Software, Provider will deposit updated source code, documentation, names, and contact information with the Escrow Agent. ("Deposit Material" refers to material required to be deposited pursuant to this Subsection ___(b).)

(c) *Verification.* At Recipient's request and expense, the Escrow Agent may at any time verify the Deposit Material, including without limitation by compiling source code, running tests to compare it to the Software, and reviewing the completeness and accuracy of any and all material. In the event that the Escrow Agent informs the parties that the Deposit Material does not conform to the requirements of Subsection ___(b) above: (i) Provider will promptly deposit conforming Deposit Material; and (ii) Provider will reimburse Recipient for subsequent verification of the new Deposit Material (except to the extent that subsequent verification exceeds the cost of the unsuccessful verification by more than ___ %). Any breach of the provisions of Subsection ___(c)(i) above will constitute material breach of this Agreement, and no further payments will be due from Recipient until such breach is cured, in addition to such other remedies as Recipient may have.

should try to require deposit of "all documentation necessary to enable a person of reasonable skill with software to compile and build machine-readable code for the Software, to maintain the Software, and to fully operate the Software."

Recipients should also consider adding employee contact information to the escrow material. No one understands software better than its authors, and the recipient might want to hire them if the provider stops providing maintenance.[10] Subsection (b) in the clause box gives the recipient contact information for the programmers. (In a larger application, the language might limit itself to certain key programmers.) Of course, programmer contact information doesn't necessarily have to pass through the escrow. If the information isn't sensitive, the provider might just hand it over.

What if the provider deposits inadequate material? The recipient won't know what's been deposited unless and until it gets its hands on the material—after a release condition. By then, the provider will probably be out of business, or at least uncooperative, and it'll be too late to insist on compliance. That's why many escrow clauses include verification procedures, as in Subsection (c). The escrow agent checks to see if the provider deposited the right material. This verification system is another reason to hire a professional escrow company, rather than use a trusty friend. Verification can be a big job, requiring significant technical expertise and resources.

2. License and Confidentiality

If the recipient does someday receive source code and other deposit material, it will need the right to exploit them. In other words, it will need a license.

In some cases, the contract's license clause already provides the necessary rights. If the software licensed—the "Licensed Product," or whatever—includes all elements of the code and documentation, including source code and other deposit material, no additional license is necessary. If not, the recipient will need a separate license, like the one in the following clause box. The license should include the same terms as the license to the underlying software, except that if the recipient is going to handle its own maintenance and support, it may also need the right to create derivative works. The source code

---

10. If the contract has a non-solicitation clause, it might interfere with the recipient's plan to hire the employees. So you might need to revise it. See Subchapter II.O.1.

Escrow License

(d) *License & Use.* Provider hereby grants Recipient a license to use, reproduce, and create derivative works from the Deposit Material, provided Recipient may not distribute or sublicense the Deposit Material or make any use of it whatsoever except for such internal use as is necessary to maintain and support the Software. Copies of the Deposit Material created or transferred pursuant to this Agreement are licensed, not sold, and Recipient receives no title to or ownership of any copy or of the Deposit Material itself. The Deposit Material constitutes Confidential Information of Provider pursuant to Section __ (*Nondisclosure*) of this Agreement (provided no provision of Section __ calling for return of Confidential Information before termination of this Agreement will apply to the Deposit Material).

---

license also needs some or all of the same restrictions as the underlying software license.[11]

The license should be effective immediately, even though the recipient doesn't yet have access to the source code and may never get it. In other words, don't write: "Upon the occurrence of a Release Condition, Provider grants Recipient a license . . ." If the provider goes bankrupt, it can rescind such a license. The only license that can reliably survive bankruptcy is one that's effective *before* bankruptcy proceedings start. That's why the example above provides: "Provider *hereby* grants Recipient a license . . ." That license is effective immediately. (For additional language addressing licenses and bankruptcy, see Chapter III.M.)

Keep in mind: the fact that the license is effective immediately doesn't mean the recipient can use the source code immediately. It has the legal right to do so, but it doesn't have a *copy*. The escrow agent has the source code and won't give it to the recipient unless and until a release condition occurs.

Providers should make sure the license limits the recipient's rights to deposit material. After all, if the provider comes out of

---

11. See Chapter I.A ("Standard End User Software License") and Subchapter I.C.1 ("Copyright License Rights").

bankruptcy, or recovers from whatever kept it from supporting the software, it will still want to protect its source code. So the license should limit the recipient to internal use: it can only use the source code to support and maintain the software, as in the previous example.

Providers should make sure the recipient protects the secrecy of the source code. If the contract has a nondisclosure clause, the deposit material should be considered confidential information, as in the previous example.[12] And if there is no nondisclosure clause, the escrow clause should include some kind of confidentiality provision. For instance, here's a short one: "The Deposit Material includes trade secrets of Provider, and Recipient will not disclose it to any third party except to the extent required by law."

3. Release and Other Issues

What triggers release of material to the recipient? Any event can serve, but release conditions usually fall into two categories: (1) the provider has breached its obligation to support the software; and (2) the provider is going out of business. (In some deals, the release conditions appear in the escrow agreement, rather than the main contract.)

The provider should make sure the contract talks about "material" breaches of support obligations, not just any technical breach. It should also make sure a breach doesn't count as a release condition unless it goes uncorrected for some period of time, like thirty days. See Subsection (e)(i) in the following clause box.

Providers might argue that the only necessary release condition is breach of the maintenance obligation. After all, the recipient doesn't need the source code or other materials if the provider continues maintaining the system, even if it does file bankruptcy or otherwise faces business trouble. So release conditions (e)(ii) through (e)(v) aren't necessary, the argument goes. But these "business trouble" release conditions are common, because providers usually *do* stop providing maintenance soon after any of these going-out-of-business warning signs. Recipients don't want to risk delays in accessing crucial source code. As with all contract debates, resolution will probably come down to leverage.[13]

---

12. See Chapter II.H ("Nondisclosure/Confidentiality").

13. The provider's bankruptcy may not be an enforceable release condition, though it appears in most escrow clauses.

Escrow Release Conditions

(e) *Release Conditions.* The term "Release Conditions," as used in the Escrow Agreement, refers to any of the following: (i) material breach by Provider of Subsection __(b) (*Maintenance*) of this Agreement, if such breach remains uncured ___ or more days after Recipient's written notice; (ii) any failure of Provider to function as a going concern; (iii) appointment, application for, or consent to a receiver, trustee, or other custodian for Provider or its assets; (iv) Provider becomes insolvent or unable to pay its debts as they mature in the ordinary course or makes an assignment for the benefit of creditors; or (v) Provider is liquidated or dissolved, or any proceedings are commenced with regard to Provider under any bankruptcy, insolvency, or debtor's relief law.

What if, at some point, the recipient tells the escrow agent a release condition has occurred, and the provider disagrees? The escrow agent is caught in the middle. Usually, it's the escrow agreement that solves this problem, with an arbitration clause. In case of dispute, the escrow agent doesn't have to release the material until it gets an order from an arbitrator. That's a good solution, but it can cause problems for the recipient if the software is critical and urgently needs maintenance. So recipients should consider a contract clause calling for *expedited* arbitration: a very fast procedure available through many arbitration associations.[14]

Finally, the escrow agreement—rather than the license agreement—should usually include a termination clause. It should provide that, if the license agreement is terminated for any reason, other than breach by the provider, the escrow agent will return the escrow material to the provider.

H. Nondisclosure / Confidentiality

In a nondisclosure clause, one party commits to keep the other's sensitive information confidential. These clauses can appear in al-

---

14. See Chapter II.S ("Alternate Dispute Resolution").

most any IT contract, but they're most common in services agreements. A nondisclosure clause can also serve as the central provision in a separate nondisclosure agreement (NDA).

A nondisclosure clause may operate in both directions or only one. In a one-way clause, one party discloses confidential information and the other receives it and keeps it secret. In a two-way or "mutual" clause, either party may disclose or receive confidential information. Usually, two-way clauses call the parties "Disclosing Party" and "Receiving Party," or something like that.[15] Those names aren't attached to one party but rather rotate, depending on who's disclosing and who's receiving at any given moment. This chapter uses them the same way.

The examples in this chapter are two-way clauses. If you'd like to use them for a one-way provision, delete the definitions of "Disclosing Party" and "Receiving Party" in the first clause box (page 79). Then, throughout the clause, replace those terms with whatever names you're using for your parties ("Provider," "Recipient," "Distributor," etc.).

You should be aware that the law provides protection for certain sensitive information even if it's not covered by a nondisclosure clause. A "trade secret" is information that's (a) valuable because it's not widely known or easily discovered by people who could use it and (b) subject to reasonable efforts to maintain secrecy.[16] Trade secret infringement is against the law even without a contract. But trade secrets law only protects against *unauthorized* taking or use of information. If the disclosing party *gives* the information without any contractual or other restriction, trade secrets law won't help. So nondisclosure clauses play a role in trade secrets protection by defining authorized and unauthorized use.

Finally, don't confuse nondisclosure clauses with data security clauses, addressed in the next chapter (specifically, Subchapter II.I.2). Data security clauses address *procedures* for protecting data, while most nondisclosure clauses simply forbid disclosure and say little or nothing about procedures for preventing it. Also, data security clauses address data in electronic form, whether sensitive or not,

---

15. Don't confuse "receiving party" with "recipient," the term used in this book for the licensee, transferee, or customer.

16. This definition paraphrases the Uniform Trade Secrets Act, adopted in most states.

while nondisclosure clauses address information in any form (paper, oral, electronic, etc.), and only sensitive information. In some cases, you'll have both nondisclosure and data security terms in your contract—sometimes covering the same information. For instance, you might have a nondisclosure clause forbidding disclosure of certain confidential information and a data security clause requiring firewalls and other systems to protect electronic data. If the confidential information includes documents in electronic form, both clauses would cover those documents. Don't let the overlap throw you off. These are separate clauses.[17]

1. What's Confidential?

Many clauses define "Confidential Information" as "any nonpublic, sensitive, or private information disclosed by the Disclosing Party." That's not a good definition because there's so much room for dispute about what's "sensitive or private." The following isn't much better: "The Software, the Documentation, and any and all information regarding the Software are 'Confidential Information.'" The software itself is confidential? Does that mean the receiving party can't let visitors see screenshots? Is the very fact that the receiving party *uses* the software confidential? In general, scorched-earth definitions serve little purpose because they don't provide clear guidance.

The clearest clauses require that the disclosing party *mark* sensitive documents "Confidential," as in Subsection (a)(i) in the following clause box. In many contracts, that's enough. (But then the disclosing party has to remember—has to actually mark sensitive documents.) In some relationships, however, confidential information will be disclosed orally: "OK, what I'm gonna tell you next is confidential, per the contract." Because memories aren't reliable, the clause should require that the disclosing party confirm the designation in writing, as in Subsection (a)(ii).

Note that any clause that lets the disclosing party decide what's confidential creates a risk for the receiving party. The disclosing party could designate too much. It could disclose confidential infor-

---

17. Some contract drafters use nondisclosure clauses to address data security. That leads to confusion and errors because of the differences noted previously. For more on this issue, see Subchapter II.I.2 ("Data Security").

Confidential Information Definition

(a) *Confidential Information.* "Confidential Information" refers to the following items one party to this Agreement (the "Disclosing Party") discloses to the other (the "Receiving Party"): (i) any document the Disclosing Party marks "Confidential"; (ii) any information the Disclosing Party orally designates as "Confidential" at the time of disclosure, provided the Disclosing Party confirms such designation in writing within ___ business days; and (iii) any source code for the Software disclosed by Provider, whether or not marked as confidential. Notwithstanding the foregoing, Confidential Information does not include information that: (A) is in the Receiving Party's possession at the time of disclosure; (B) is independently developed by the Receiving Party without use of or reference to Confidential Information; (C) becomes known publicly, before or after disclosure, other than as a result of the Receiving Party's improper action or inaction; or (D) is approved for release in writing by the Disclosing Party.

mation the receiving party doesn't want—information that will be hard to protect or that might restrict the receiving party's business. If this risk is high (e.g., because of low trust), the clause could include a safety valve: "Before disclosure, the Disclosing Party will provide the Receiving Party with a nonconfidential written summary of any data intended to be Confidential Information. Within 5 business days of receipt of such a summary, the Receiving Party may reject the information in writing. Information disclosed without such a summary, or after such rejection, will not be considered Confidential Information."

The other way to designate confidential information is to "pre-mark" it: to identify certain types of sensitive data in advance, in the contract. Subsection (a)(iii) in the clause box pre-marks source code. The key, as always, is clarity: leave no doubt as to what information is confidential.

Whatever the definition of confidential information, some data should be excluded. The example above excludes the key types: data the receiving party already has or develops independently, and data that's already public.

2. Restrictions on Use

The core terms of a nondisclosure clause tell the receiving party what *not* to do with confidential information. There are many ways to put it, but in short, the receiving party can't pass the information on to third parties without permission.

The example in the following clause box has three key directives. First, the receiving party won't use the confidential information for anything but the transaction outlined in the agreement. Second, the receiving party won't give confidential information to anyone not authorized. And third, the receiving party will take reasonable steps to protect the information. That three-part structure is common but not required. Some clauses simply forbid disclosure to anyone unauthorized and leave it at that.

The example in the clause box requires that the receiving party have its employees sign NDAs if they get access to Confidential information. That's not always necessary. Often the disclosing party can rely on the receiving party's supervision of employees. If you do need separate NDAs, you can take the clause box examples in this chapter and put them into a separate contract between the employee and the receiving party. (Note that in some cases, the disclosing party wants to sign the employee NDA too, or wants to sign instead of the receiving party.) The NDA usually won't need any other terms except boilerplate clauses, addressed in Part III of this book.[18]

A nondisclosure clause doesn't have to address standards for protecting confidential information. Those that do usually require "reasonable care" or something similar, like the example in the following clause box. But there's nothing to keep you from drafting more detailed standards or procedures. For example: "The Receiving Party will keep all copies of Confidential Information in a locked safe at its corporate headquarters, with keys or combinations available only to its General Counsel. The Receiving Party will shred all copies of documents containing Confidential Information promptly after use."

---

18. The forms library at this book's website includes a sample NDA you can use for the receiving party's employees. Please visit www.TechContractsHandbook.com.

Nondisclosure

(b) *Nondisclosure.* The Receiving Party will not use Confidential Information for any purpose other than to facilitate the transactions contemplated by this Agreement (the "Purpose"). The Receiving Party: (i) will not disclose Confidential Information to any employee or contractor of the Receiving Party unless such person needs access in order to facilitate the Purpose and executes a nondisclosure agreement with the Receiving Party, with terms no less restrictive than those of this Section __; and (ii) will not disclose Confidential Information to any other third party without the Disclosing Party's prior written consent. Without limiting the generality of the foregoing, the Receiving Party will protect Confidential Information with the same degree of care it uses to protect its own confidential information of similar nature and importance, but with no less than reasonable care. The Receiving Party will promptly notify the Disclosing Party of any misuse or misappropriation of Confidential Information that comes to the Receiving Party's attention. Notwithstanding the foregoing, the Receiving Party may disclose Confidential Information as required by applicable law or by proper legal or governmental authority. The Receiving Party will give the Disclosing Party prompt notice of any such legal or governmental demand and reasonably cooperate with the Disclosing Party in any effort to seek a protective order or otherwise to contest such required disclosure, at the Disclosing Party's expense.

(If the confidential information includes electronic data and you impose standards for protecting it, you're stepping partway into the data security clause's territory. See Subchapter II.I.2 ("Data Security").)

Finally, most nondisclosure clauses—including the example above—allow the receiving party to share confidential information with the government and with courts (including litigants with discovery rights) to the extent required by law. That's a necessary exception.

3. *Injunction, Termination, and Retention of Rights*

Most nondisclosure clauses give the disclosing party the right to a court-issued injunction against leaks. And most also address termination of the agreement and "ownership" of information.

If the receiving party leaks the confidential information or threatens to leak it, the disclosing party will probably want to plug the leak before it's too late. It needs a court order or "injunction" directing the receiving party to protect the information. If the contract doesn't address this injunction issue and the parties wind up in court, the receiving party could argue that the disclosing party doesn't really need an injunction—that money damages, granted after the fact, would be enough. To defeat that argument, Subsection (c) in the clause box below has the receiving party admit in advance that money

---

Injunction, Termination, and Retention of Rights

(c) *Injunction.* The Receiving Party agrees that breach of this Section __ might cause the Disclosing Party irreparable injury, for which monetary damages would not provide adequate compensation, and that in addition to any other remedy, the Disclosing Party will be entitled to injunctive relief against such breach or threatened breach, without proving actual damage or posting a bond or other security.

(d) *Termination and Return.* The obligations of Subsection __ (b) above (*Nondisclosure*) will terminate _____ after the Effective Date. Upon termination of this Agreement, the Receiving Party will return all copies of Confidential Information to the Disclosing Party or certify, in writing, the destruction thereof.

(e) *Retention of Rights.* This Section __ does not transfer ownership of Confidential Information or grant a license thereto. Except to the extent that another section of this Agreement specifically provides to the contrary, the Disclosing Party will retain all right, title, and interest in and to all Confidential Information.

---

damages wouldn't do the trick. The leak would injure the disclosing party's business in a way that no amount of money could compensate.

Subsection (d) of the clause box puts a time limit on nondisclosure obligations. Keeping secrets can be burdensome, and most secrets grow less sensitive over time. So nondisclosure clauses usually fix an end date for the receiving party's obligations. In six months, five years, or whenever, the receiving party is off the hook. Subsection (d) sets a consistent end date for all confidential information, but you might instead provide that nondisclosure obligations terminate "three years after disclosure of the item of Confidential Information in question." And of course, you don't need any expiration date, if you think your confidential information will remain sensitive indefinitely. If so, delete the first sentence of Subsection (d).

Finally, whenever the obligations terminate, the disclosing party should consider terms requiring return or destruction of confidential documents after the relationship ends, and confirming that the contract doesn't grant a license to confidential information, or transfer ownership. See Subsection (e) and the last sentence of Subsection (d). Some confidentiality clauses also require return of confidential information on the disclosing party's request.

I. Data Management and Security

Data management and data security clauses address information in electronic form. They appear most often in services contracts. They may also appear in software license agreements where the provider offers maintenance, tech support, or other services.[19]

In some services deals, the provider gets access to data on the recipient's computers—through an electronic connection between offices for instance, or by sending technicians to the recipient's office. In others, the provider collects or stores data for the recipient—through an online software application for instance (software as a service). Either type of deal may call for data management and security terms.

---

19. See Chapters I.E ("Programming, Maintenance, Consulting, and Other Professional Services") and I.F ("Software as a Service and Other Machine-Based Services").

1. Data Management and E-Discovery

Data management clauses address the recipient's right to control its data—to access and copy it, and to require that the provider retain or erase it. They apply to providers that store recipient data, or at least host it temporarily. They generally don't fit providers that get access to data but don't ever host it.

Most large companies operate under data management policies, addressing questions like how long the company will retain electronic data and when it will erase that data. These policies may also address "e-discovery." If the company finds itself in court, other litigants may issue discovery demands for access to its records, including electronic data. Once the company anticipates a lawsuit, it will need to place a "litigation hold" on its data, to make sure nothing relevant to the case gets erased. (Erasing relevant data can lead to court-imposed sanctions.) Obviously, these policies become complicated if a third party holds the data. So data management clauses require that providers follow recipients' data policies and instructions.

The example in the following clause box fits best in a deal involving "high touch" services—where the provider can mold its policies to the recipient's needs, at least to some extent. If the provider offers a standardized service, that kind of flexibility may not be possible. Many software as a service providers, for instance, manage recipient data according to their own policies and can't easily accommodate the kind of data handling requests authorized by the example. So your data management clause may need to go easier on the provider.

Subsection (b) of the clause box confirms the recipient's ownership of the data—or at least confirms that the provider has no rights to the data and only acts as the recipient's agent. The subsection also calls on the provider to give the recipient access to the data and to allow copying. Copying may be important for e-discovery if litigants send the provider e-discovery demands for the recipient's data. Usually, neither party wants that. The provider doesn't want the expense and hassle of complying with e-discovery demands, and the recipient wants to control the discovery process by providing the data itself. If the recipient has a copy of all data in the provider's possession, it can tell the litigants and the court that there's nothing to be gained from e-discovery directed to the provider.

The method of data access and copying will depend on the type and quantity of data and on the parties' technical abilities. The "Data Access Rules" referenced in Subsection (b) might call for CDs

Data Management

(a) *Access, Use, & Legal Compulsion.* Unless it receives Recipient's prior written consent, Provider: (i) will not access or use data in electronic form collected through the Services from Recipient's customers or other third parties, or collected or accessible directly from Recipient, (collectively, "Project Data") other than as necessary to facilitate the Services; and (ii) will not give any third party access to Project Data. Notwithstanding the foregoing, Provider may disclose Project Data as required by applicable law or by proper legal or governmental authority. Provider will give Recipient prompt notice of any such legal or governmental demand and reasonably cooperate with Recipient in any effort to seek a protective order or otherwise to contest such required disclosure, at Recipient's expense.

(b) *Recipient's Rights.* Recipient possesses and retains all right, title, and interest in and to Project Data, and Provider's use and possession thereof is solely as Recipient's agent. Recipient may access and copy any Project Data in Provider's possession at any time, through the media of communication described on the data access rules attached to this Agreement as Attachment __. Provider will facilitate such access and copying promptly after Recipient's request.

(c) *Retention & Deletion.* Provider will retain any Project Data in its possession until Erased (as defined below) pursuant to this Subsection __(c). Provider will Erase: (i) all copies of Project Data _____ after collection thereof; (ii) any or all copies of Project Data promptly after Recipient's written request; and (iii) all copies of Project Data no sooner than __ business days after termination of this Agreement and no later than __ business days after such termination. Notwithstanding the foregoing, Recipient may at any time instruct Provider to retain and not to Erase or otherwise delete Project Data, provided Recipient may not require retention of Project Data for more than __ business days after termination of this Agreement. Promptly after Erasure pursuant to this Subsection __ (c), Provider will certify such Erasure in writing to Recipient. ("Erase" and "Erasure" refer to the destruction of data so that no copy of the data remains or can be accessed or restored in any way.)

dropped in the mail, a VPN (virtual private network) connection, or almost anything else.

Subsection (b) in the previous clause box doesn't say anything about returning data to the recipient. Often, one party's copy is just as good as another, so there's no reason for any "return" of data. But in some cases a particular copy (e.g., the original) may have some value, so a return requirement would make sense.

Subsection (c) of the clause box lays out the recipient's basic data management policies and requires that the provider obey them.[20] It includes the recipient's right to stop any routine data deletion, in case of a litigation hold (or for other reasons). Instead of imposing requirements in the contract itself, however, Subsection (c) could provide: "Provider will comply with recipient's standard data management policy, attached to this Agreement as Exhibit A. Recipient may revise such policy from time to time by providing a new version of Exhibit A to Provider." With language like that, providers should consider placing some limits on policy revisions, to make sure data management doesn't become too expensive.

A data management clause generally shouldn't tell the provider to "delete" data. Definitions vary, but deletion often does nothing more than move data to a virtual recycle bin. The information remains on the computer and can be restored. "Erase" is a better word, but even there definitions can vary. The best plan is to define erasure, leaving no doubt that the provider must destroy the data so that no one can ever access it again. See the last sentence of Subsection (c) in the previous clause box.

The example in the previous clause box fits providers that store recipient data, as well as those that access data but don't store or host it. The example's "Project Data" definition, for instance, includes data merely "accessible" from the recipient. As this subchapter's first paragraph explains, data management clauses aren't necessary for providers that merely access data without hosting or storing it. The example addresses "mere access" because the same example continues below, in the data security subchapter—and data security provisions *are* necessary for "mere access."

---

20. Subsection (c) includes a time line for erasing data after the contract terminates. You should fill in the blanks so that erasure takes place during a defined period: "Provider will Erase all Project Data no sooner than 20 business days after termination of this Agreement and no later than 35 business days after such termination." That way, the recipient knows the earliest date the provider can start erasing—and can delay it if necessary—and also knows when erasure will be done.

2. Data Security

Data security clauses address sensitive electronic data. They apply to providers that store or host recipient data, as well as those that merely access it, or could access it. They require that the provider protect the data from theft or other exposure. That's particularly important if the data includes private information, like customer names, addresses, or social security numbers.

If your deal involves electronic data that's not private or otherwise sensitive, you don't need a data security clause. The data management terms in Subchapter 1 should cover all your needs.

Don't confuse data security clauses with nondisclosure clauses or agreements (NDAs), addressed in Chapter II.H. The two have some similar terms but different purposes. Nondisclosure clauses forbid disclosure of certain information but generally say little or nothing about procedures for protecting that information. Data security clauses, on the other hand, focus on procedures. Also, nondisclosure clauses can address information in any form—paper, oral, electronic, etc.—and only cover sensitive information. Data security clauses cover electronic data only, and they generally don't distinguish between sensitive and nonsensitive data. (It's not usually practical to separate sensitive information from the rest of a database.)

Your deal might call for both a nondisclosure clause and a data security clause, and some of your information might be covered by both. For instance, the recipient might give the provider electronic copies of secret business plans, covered by the nondisclosure clause, and those copies might get stored with the rest of the recipient's data on the provider's computers, covered by the data security clause. Or your data security clause might require that the provider's employees sign NDAs covering electronic data. (See the following.) Don't let the potential overlap confuse you. These are separate clauses.[21]

Like the example clause in Subchapter 1, the example in the following clause box is most appropriate for deals involving "high touch"

---

21. Or at least they should be, in my opinion. Data security is a newer concept than nondisclosure, and the legal community hasn't entirely figured out how to handle it. Many lawyers graft data security provisions onto nondisclosure clauses, and some include electronic data in the NDA definition of "Confidential Information," whether it's sensitive or not. In my experience, those blended clauses come riddled with errors, unless drafted by an expert, and cause confusion. To solve the problem, I've more or less made up the concept of an entirely separate data security clause, though most likely I'm not the first to do so. You probably *will* run into contracts with blended clauses. This chapter should help you cut through any resulting confusion.

Data Security

(d) *Technical & Physical Security.* In its handling of Project Data, Provider will observe the Technical and Physical Security Requirements attached to this Agreement as Attachment __.

(e) *Individuals' Access.* Provider will not allow any of its employees to access Project Data, except to the extent that an employee needs access in order to facilitate the Services and executes a written agreement with Provider agreeing to comply with Provider's obligations set forth in this Section __. Provider will perform a background check on any individual it gives access to Project Data. Such background check will include, without limitation, a review of the individual's criminal history, if any. Provider will not grant access to Project Data if the background check or other information in Provider's possession would lead a reasonable person to suspect that the individual has committed identity theft or otherwise misused third party data or that the individual presents a threat to the security of Project Data.

(f) *Compliance with Law & Policy.* Provider will comply with all applicable federal and state laws and regulations governing the handling of Project Data.

(g) *Testing & Audits.* Recipient may test Provider's Project Data management systems _____ times per _____, including without limitation via unannounced penetration tests, and Provider will cooperate with such tests as Recipient reasonably requests. No less than once per calendar year, Provider will retain a certified public accounting firm (i) to perform a SAS-70 audit that includes Provider's Project Data management systems and (ii) to produce a SAS-70 Type II report. Provider will provide such report to Recipient promptly after receipt thereof, and such report will be considered Confidential Information disclosed by Provider pursuant to Section __ (*Nondisclosure*) of this Agreement.

(h) *Leaks.* Provider will promptly notify Recipient of any actual or potential exposure or misappropriation of Project Data (any "Leak") that comes to Provider's attention. Provider will cooperate with Recipient and with law enforcement authorities in investigating any such Leak, at Provider's expense. Provider will likewise cooperate with Recipient and with law enforcement agencies in any effort to notify injured or potentially injured parties, and such cooperation will be at Provider's expense, except to the extent that the Leak was caused by Recipient. The remedies and obligations set forth in this Subsection __(h) are in addition to any others Recipient may have.

(i) *Injunction.* Provider agrees that violation of the provisions of this Section __ might cause Recipient irreparable injury, for which monetary damages would not provide adequate compensation, and that in addition to any other remedy, Recipient will be entitled to injunctive relief against such breach or threatened breach, without proving actual damage or posting a bond or other security.

services—where the provider can mold its policies to the recipient's needs. For more standardized services, you'll probably need to pare back some of the provider obligations listed in the clause box.

In a sense, the example in the clause box provides the skeleton of a data security clause. The flesh comes from the technical and physical security requirements, referenced in Subsection (d). They address IT-related protection, like encryption and passwords. Like software technical specifications, the technical and physical requirements might be drafted by either party's IT staff, but whoever's ultimately responsible for the deal—lawyer, contract manager, IT manager, etc.—should review them and make sure they're clear and complete. Drafting technical and physical security requirements lies outside the scope of this book, but for suggestions on creating and editing technical documents in general, see Subchapters II.A.2 ("Responsibility for Specifications") and II.A.3 ("Organizing and Editing Specifications").

In addition to technical and physical requirements, a data security clause might reference the recipient's privacy policy: its rules for handling private information. "In its handling of Protected Data, Provider will comply with the requirements of Recipient's privacy policy, attached to this Agreement as Attachment B." Privacy policies vary, but many address topics like use of private data for marketing, as well as disclosure to subcontractors and other third parties.[22]

Subsection (e) in the clause box requires that the provider have its employees sign written contracts promising to protect the data.[23] Obviously, that's only necessary for the most sensitive data. The employee contract could be an NDA (addressed in Chapter II.H), with "all Recipient's electronic data" added to the definition of "Confidential Information." You might also add the following to an employee NDA, or have employees sign a separate contract that provides: "Employee will comply with and support compliance with all Provider's obligations set forth in Section __ (*Data Security*) of the Services Agreement between Provider and Recipient, attached to this Agreement as Exhibit A." (If you use that language, you should attach the underlying contract to the NDA or other employee agreement, or somehow make the contract available, because employees can't comply with data security requirements they haven't seen.)

Various laws and regulations impose data security standards on companies that handle private data.[24] In Subsection (f) of the clause box (page 88), the provider promises to obey those laws. So if the provider violates some legal rule on data security, it's liable to the recipient for breach of contract, on top of potential liability to consumers and the government. This double (or triple) liability makes the most sense where the provider offers services specifically tailored to the recipient's industry or to the type of data in question. But even there, the provider might refuse Subsection (f), particularly if it's not equipped to keep up with changes in the law. Or the provider might promise "reasonable efforts" to comply with the law.

Subsection (g) of the clause box addresses testing: procedures for determining the quality of the provider's security systems. The

---

22. For privacy policies used by websites and online services, see Appendix 5.

23. The example requires a contract for employees, not for independent contractors, on the assumption that contractors won't have any access to the data. In the clause box in Subchapter II.I.1, Subsection (a)(ii) tells the provider not to give data to third parties. That would include contractors.

24. The federal government's key data security laws include the Gramm-Leach-Bliley Act (governing financial institutions), the Health Insurance Portability and Accountability Act, the Children's Online Privacy Protection Act, and arguably the Sarbanes-Oxley Act (on corporate corruption and financial reporting). Most states have information privacy laws and regulations too. Massachusetts has some of the most far-reaching regulations, codified at 201 CMR 17.00.

first sentence lets the recipient test those systems itself, including by trying to hack into the provider's computers. Obviously, that doesn't make sense in all deals. The second sentence calls on the provider to perform "SAS-70" audits: a common system stability audit described in Subchapter II.R.1 ("Financial and Technical Reporting").

If the provider fails to protect the data, the recipient will probably want to plug the leak as soon as possible. It needs a court order or "injunction" directing the provider to protect the information. If the contract doesn't address this injunction issue and the parties wind up in court, the receiving party could argue that the disclosing party doesn't need an injunction—that money damages granted after the fact will be enough. To defeat that argument, Subsection (i) of the clause box has the receiving party admit in advance that money damages wouldn't do the trick. The leak would injure the disclosing party's business in a way that no amount of money could compensate.

In addition to the protections in the clause box, the recipient might want warranty or indemnity terms addressing data security. For instance: "Provider warrants that its data security systems comply with the Technical and Physical Security Requirements. Provider will indemnify and defend Recipient from any loss arising out of or related to any breach of the warranty in the previous sentence." Obviously, those terms would impose serious risks on the provider.[25]

J. Warranty

A warranty promises that something is true or will happen. It's a guarantee. A warranty can cover any topic, and it can come from either the recipient or the provider, though you'll see provider warranties more often.

IT contracts offer a variety of warranties, particularly promises that software or other goods will work, at least for a certain period, and guarantees of the provider's right to transfer IP. Most IT contracts also *disclaim* certain warranties. Finally, many contracts specify remedies for breach of warranty.

In most IT contracts, one party "represents and warrants" some set of facts. Technically speaking, those two terms have different meanings. A "representation" is a statement of present fact, while a

---

25. See Chapters II.J ("Warranty") and II.K ("Indemnity").

"warranty" is a promise that something will be true in the future. But that distinction plays no role in modern contract drafting. As used today, both representations and warranties state facts offered to convince a party to enter into a contract. So you're just repeating yourself if you use both terms, and you should choose one. I recommend "warrant" because IT professionals expect it. If your contract offers a set of representations, the other party will inevitably complain: "Where are my warranties?"[26]

Warranty clauses are common for both software and services contracts.

1. Warranty of Function

The warranty of function promises that software will "work."

What does it mean to warrant that software or services will work? A clear warranty clause refers to the contract's technical specifications, as in the first example in the following clause box. In other words, the warranty says that the software will perform as required in the technical specs attached to the contract.[27]

Unfortunately, warranties of function are often much less clear. For instance: "Provider warrants that the Software will be in good working order." Ugh. What does that mean? A slight improvement might read that the system will "perform according to its documentation." But what is documentation? Brochures, e-mails from salespeople, ads posted online . . . ? If you're going to reference documentation that isn't attached to the contract, state which documents you mean. For instance, the provider might put a label or stamp on official documentation, as in the following second example. That clause is adequate, assuming the provider is careful to stamp "Official Product Documentation" in the appropriate places—and assuming there can be no doubt which documents qualify, those documents are clear, and they explain what the product is supposed to do (like technical specs).

---

26. Representations and warranties do play different roles in litigation. A false representation gives rise to a claim of misrepresentation, while a false warranty gives rise to a claim of breach of warranty. The two arise under different laws and have different consequences. But the litigation distinction isn't dependent on whether the contract uses the term "represent" or "warrant." A statement described as a representation can give rise to a breach of warranty claim, while a statement described as a warranty can give rise to a misrepresentation claim. In other words, the nature of the claim depends on the context (on issues outside the scope of this discussion), not on the choice of words.

27. See Chapter II.A ("Technical Specifications").

Warranty of Function

Provider warrants that, during the _____ period following delivery, the Software will perform materially as described in the technical specifications set forth in Exhibit A.

• • • •

Provider warrants that, during the first _____ after installation, each New Module will perform according to its documentation issued by Provider under the heading "Official Product Documentation."

The provider can warrant just about anything in terms of functionality. Some warranties are customized and address the particular needs of the deal. For instance: "Provider warrants that no Deliverable, when installed, will impair the System's ability to process purchase and sales transactions at the speeds set forth in Exhibit C."

Providers often qualify warranties of function by requiring only "material" conformity with specs or with other requirements, as in the first example in the clause box. If every glitch counted as a breach of warranty, the provider would be in trouble. The use of "material" excludes unimportant errors.

Finally, warranties of function usually have time limits, as in both examples above. If the system stops working the day after the warranty expires (as required by Murphy's Law), the provider is off the hook. But a time limit isn't required. The provider could warrant the system indefinitely or "during the term of this Agreement."

If the warranty does include a time limit, the recipient should think about when the warranty *starts*. If the provider is installing software or customizing it, the warranty probably shouldn't start until the job is done. While the provider's hard at work on getting the software installed and working, the recipient doesn't need a separate promise that the system will work. If the system fails, the provider already has to deal with it. That's why the last clause provides that the warranty continues for X period "after installation." Even better for the recipient, the warranty might continue for X period "after Acceptance of the final Deliverable."[28]

---

28. For acceptance, see Chapter II.F.

2. Infringement/Ownership Warranty

The infringement or ownership warranty guarantees property rights, particularly rights in intellectual property. It promises that no third party will come along and keep the recipient from using the software through a claim that it infringes some copyright or other IP right. In other words, the provider is saying, "We guarantee we have the authority to license these IP rights." Infringement warranties are appropriate for nearly all software contracts.

Some providers balk at the IP side of the ownership warranty: "How can we guarantee that? There are millions of patents covering all kinds of technologies. How can we possibly be sure our product doesn't infringe one of them?" The answer is that the provider *can't* be sure. Nor can most providers be sure their engineers didn't illegally copy a few lines of code, infringing someone's copyright. But providers don't need to be sure because the warranty isn't about certainty. It's about *allocation of risk*. The typical IP warranty says that the provider, not the recipient, bears the legal risk that the goods infringe some third party's IP. That's often appropriate because it's *the provider's* product. The provider is in a better position to create safeguards: to do a patent search, to hire engineers who are honest and careful, etc.

That's not to say the provider has to accept the risk. It can refuse to guarantee IP rights or other ownership rights. Or it can simply warrant that it doesn't *know* of any IP infringement, limiting its risk. "Provider warrants that it is not aware of any copyright, patent, or other intellectual property right infringed by the Software, and that it is not aware of any claim of intellectual property infringement related to the Software."

Infringement Warranty

Provider warrants that it is the owner of the System and of each and every component thereof, or the recipient of a valid license thereto, and that it has and will maintain the full power and authority to grant the intellectual property and other rights granted in this Agreement without the further consent of any third party.

3. Other Warranties

Warranties can cover almost any topic. The examples in the clause box below are common, but you should craft whatever language fits your deal.

The third example in the clause box protects software distributors against open source software provided with a "copyleft" or "viral" license.[29] The fourth promises that services will be "workmanlike": a somewhat vague but common term meaning professional and skilled. The other examples should be self-explanatory.

Special Warranties

Each party warrants that it has the full right and authority to enter into, execute, and perform its obligations under this Agreement and that no pending or threatened claim or litigation known to it would have a material adverse impact on its ability to perform as required by this Agreement.

• • • •

Provider warrants that the Software and any media used to distribute it contain no viruses or other computer instructions or technological means intended to disrupt, damage, or interfere with the use of computers or related systems.

• • • •

Provider warrants that the Licensed Program does not include software subject to any legal requirement that would restrict Distributor's right to distribute the Licensed Program, or any modification thereof: (a) for a fee, (b) with or without source code or source code rights, or (c) with such restrictions as Distributor sees fit to place on its customers' modification or distribution rights.

• • • •

---

29. See Appendix 3 ("Open Source Software Contracts").

> Provider warrants that all Services will be performed in a workmanlike manner.
>
> • • • •
>
> Provider warrants that the Services will comply with all applicable laws, including without limitation federal, state, and local.

Remember that warranties don't truly promise a state of affairs. Rather, *they shift legal risk.* So the provider might not actually be able to guarantee that it won't deliver a computer virus, or that its services comply with every conceivable law—as in the second and last examples above. But the provider can promise to take the blame for a virus or a broken law or anything else. It can accept the legal risk.

That said, providers often refuse that legal risk; they limit their warranties to events they can control. So instead of the virus warranty in the second example in the clause box, the contract might read: "Provider warrants that it will analyze each Deliverable with the latest commercially available version of MMR Antivirus software and will not deliver any Deliverable with a virus discovered by such software or with any other computer instructions or technological means, discovered by such software, intended to disrupt, damage, or interfere with the use of computers or related systems." And instead of the legal compliance warranty in the last example, the contract might read: "Provider warrants that it has or will exercise commercially reasonable efforts, including consultation with counsel, to ensure that the Services comply with all applicable laws." A similar "reasonable efforts" warranty could be substituted for any of the previous examples.

4. Disclaimers of Warranties

Most IT warranty clauses include disclaimers. In fact, for many providers, the clause's key job is disclaiming warranties, not granting them.

Some software contracts disclaim all warranties. The software is sold "as is" or "with all faults." See the second example in the following

Warranty Disclaimers

EXCEPT FOR THE EXPRESS WARRANTIES SPECIFIED IN SECTION __, PROVIDER MAKES NO WARRANTIES, EITHER EXPRESS OR IMPLIED, INCLUDING WITHOUT LIMITATION ANY IMPLIED WARRANTY OF MERCHANTABILITY OR FITNESS FOR A PARTICULAR PURPOSE.

• • • •

RECIPIENT ACCEPTS THE SOFTWARE "AS IS," WITH NO REPRESENTATION OR WARRANTY OF ANY KIND, EXPRESS OR IMPLIED, INCLUDING WITHOUT LIMITATION IMPLIED WARRANTIES OF MERCHANTABILITY, FITNESS FOR A PARTICULAR PURPOSE, OR NONINFRINGEMENT OF INTELLECTUAL PROPERTY RIGHTS. WITHOUT LIMITING THE GENERALITY OF THE FOREGOING, PROVIDER HAS NO OBLIGATION TO INDEMNIFY OR DEFEND RECIPIENT AGAINST CLAIMS RELATED TO INFRINGEMENT OF INTELLECTUAL PROPERTY RIGHTS.

• • • •

Provider does not warrant that the Software will perform without error or that it will run without immaterial interruption. Provider provides no warranty regarding, and will have no responsibility for, any claim arising out of: (a) a modification of the Software made by anyone other than Provider, unless Provider approves such modification in writing; or (b) use of the Software in combination with any operating system not authorized in the Documentation or Specifications or with hardware or software specifically forbidden by the Documentation or Specifications.

• • • •

Provider: (a) will pass through to Recipient any warranty right it receives from a third party provider of System components not authored or manufactured by Provider ("Third Party

> Components"); and (b) will reasonably cooperate with Recipient in enforcing such rights. Provider provides no warranties, express or implied, with regard to Third Party Components, and Provider will not be liable for any failure of any Third Party Component to function as expected or intended.

clause box. That's fine in theory, but providers should be aware that it doesn't always work. If the deal seems unfair in the extreme, some courts will brush aside the "as is" provision, particularly if the recipient is a consumer.

Whether the contract disclaims all warranties or only some, it should address implied warranties. State laws impose certain warranties on sales contracts, even if the parties don't actually write those warranties into the agreement. The three implied warranties of greatest concern are the *implied warranty of merchantability*, the *implied warranty of fitness for a particular purpose*, and the *implied warranty of noninfringement*. See the first and second examples in the previous clause box.

"Merchantability" warrants, among other things, that the goods will do what they're supposed to: they're fit for their ordinary purposes. That makes sense for lamps and toasters, because everyone knows what they're supposed to do. But software and IT services have many complex functions, and reasonable minds can differ about their ordinary purposes. So providers almost always disclaim the implied warranty of merchantability.

"Fitness for a particular purpose" warrants that a product will be appropriate for the recipient's unique needs. In the IT business, the provider often doesn't fully understand the recipient's needs, or know them at all. So providers specifically disclaim the implied warranty of fitness for a particular purpose.

"Noninfringement" warrants that the product won't infringe third party intellectual property rights. It's not clear that the law actually includes an implied warranty of noninfringement. But providers should disclaim it just in case, if they want to avoid the warranty. They should also disclaim any obligation to indemnify the recipient for infringement. See the second example in the previous clause box. Obviously, many providers do warrant IP and do indemnify the recipient for IP issues. That's why the first example in the clause box lacks a noninfringement disclaimer.[30]

Disclaimers of implied warranties should be conspicuous, appearing in all caps, as in the first two examples in the previous clause box. That's because courts are often receptive to recipients' claims that they didn't understand the disclaimers' importance (particularly if the recipients are consumers).

Not all disclaimers address implied warranties. One set of "nonimplied" disclaimers relates to misuse of the Software. Providers often disclaim responsibility for the recipients' unauthorized modification of software. Providers also disclaim warranties related to recipients' use of software on an unauthorized platform or with forbidden hardware or software. See the third example in the clause box. And for intellectual property warranties, providers should consider a broad array of disclaimers, similar to those found in many IP indemnity clauses. See Subchapter II.K.2 ("Exclusions from IP Indemnity"), and consider importing the provisions listed there into your disclaimer of warranties. Or you might simply reference your indemnity disclaimers: "The intellectual property infringement warranty in this Section 7 does not apply to the extent that the infringement arises out of any of the conditions listed in Subsection 8(d) below (*Exclusions from IP Indemnity*)."

Still another common disclaimer relates to third party components. A provider might design and sell a computer system that includes hardware and software from third parties, as well as its own products. Since the provider didn't produce the third party components, it might not be able to trust them. Worse, the third parties might have given the provider a weak warranty, or none. So the provider could find itself on the hook for someone else's product, alone. The solution is to pass through any third party warranties to the

---

30. The American Law Institute (ALI), a prestigious legal advisory body, has suggested that the law includes or should include an implied indemnity against IP infringement. This suggestion is controversial. See ALI's *Principles of the Law of Software Contracts* (ALI 2010), § 3.01. See also Chapter II.K ("Indemnity").

ALI has also suggested that the law includes or should include a nondisclaimable warranty of no "hidden material defects." Like the implied IP indemnity, this suggestion is controversial. See *Principles of the Law of Software Contracts* § 3.05(b).

recipient and disclaim any other warranty on third party components, as in the last example in the clause box (page 98).

Of course, this sort of third party pass-through creates problems for the recipient. If the system doesn't work, the provider and third party manufacturer will likely blame each other and refuse responsibility. That's why many recipients argue that, if the provider *resells* the third party component, it should take responsibility for it. Otherwise, why doesn't the recipient purchase directly from the third party—for less, without the provider's markup? Recipients also argue that the whole reason for hiring a single technology integrator (the provider) is to get a single point of contact: one party responsible for the system.

Finally, providers often disclaim specific issues in the warranty clause. For instance: "Provider does not warrant the Software's interoperability with any transaction reporting system other than *BigBrother* version 7.01." Craft whatever disclaimers fit your deal.

5. *Remedies for Breach of Warranty*

A contract doesn't have to specify a remedy for breach of warranty. If it doesn't, a court will impose money damages or other solutions (or the parties will work something out in settlement negotiations). But by agreeing on the remedies in advance, the parties remove much of the element of chance.

Usually, the provider promises to repair or replace defective goods, as in the first example in the following clause box. And for infringement warranties, the provider promises it will get the recipient a license to keep using the goods, or replace them with something noninfringing, as in the second example.

But what if these strategies fail? What if the thing can't be fixed, or the provider can't afford a license and there's no suitable replacement? For the provider, the best solution is often to refund the recipient's money, take the product back, and walk away. The first example in the clause box gives the provider that right.

This refund-and-walk-away solution may leave the recipient in the lurch. Imagine the product is a bookkeeping computer system, and the recipient's already thrown away the old system. If the recipient has to stop using the new one, it has nothing, and it's in trouble—trouble a refund won't solve. That's why recipients prefer clauses like the second example in the clause box, which leaves the provider no

Remedies for Breach of Warranty

In the event of breach of the warranty in this Section __, Provider will promptly repair the Product in question or replace it with a product of substantially similar functionality, or if such attempts do not succeed after ____ days, refund all amounts paid by Recipient for such Product. The preceding sentence states Recipient's sole remedy and Provider's entire liability for breach of such warranty.

• • • •

If the Software becomes, or in either party's reasonable opinion is likely to become, the subject of any claim, suit, or proceeding arising from or alleging infringement of any intellectual property right, or in the event of any adjudication that the Software infringes any such right, Provider, at its own expense, will promptly take the following actions: (a) secure for Recipient the right to continue using the Software; or (b) replace or modify the Software to make it noninfringing, provided such modification or replacement will not materially degrade any functionality relied upon by Recipient. The remedies set forth in the preceding sentence are not exclusive of any others Recipient may have at law or in equity.

way out other than *fix or replace*. That should motivate the provider to go the extra mile looking for a solution (or at least drag the provider down with the recipient).[31]

Whether the clause permits a refund or not, *distributors* should consider terms extending warranty remedies to their customers. For instance: "Provider's obligations set forth in this Subsection 7(d) include, without limitation, repair or refund of Software provided to Distributor's customers."[32]

If the contract specifies remedies for breach of warranty, will those remedies be "exclusive"? In other words, once the provider has

---

31. Of course, if the contract has a strong limitation of liability clause, the provider still might not be very motivated to go the extra mile. See Chapter II.L.

32. See Chapter I.B ("Standard Distributor Software License").

repaired or replaced the product, can the recipient still go after money damages or some other remedy? If the contract says nothing on the subject, there's a good chance the recipient can. To make sure, recipients often include clauses like the last sentence in the second example (page 101), providing that these remedies are not "exclusive." The provider, of course, wants to limit its responsibility to the stated remedies. So the first example in the clause box provides that the remedies *are* exclusive.

K. Indemnity

In an indemnity clause, one party promises to protect the other from lawsuits—to pay any judgments or settlements. Most IT indemnity clauses also include a *defense* provision, requiring that the responsible party—the "indemnitor"—hire attorneys and pay their fees. Indemnity clauses are appropriate for all kinds of software and IT services contracts.

Which party should give an indemnity, and for what? There is no standard answer, but in general, indemnity clauses crop up in deals involving troubling legal risks that one party can manage or mitigate while the other can't. Software deals, for instance, involve intellectual property risks. Someone might sue one or both parties, claiming use of the software infringes a patent, copyright, or other IP right. That's a risk the provider can manage, by trying to develop software that doesn't infringe. After all, it's the provider's product. The recipient, on the other hand, has very little power to manage or mitigate that risk. So software providers typically indemnify recipients against IP infringement claims.

Usually, the provider is the indemnitor, because the provider creates risks for the recipient (or distributor). That's the case with the examples in the following clause boxes. But there's no reason the provider shouldn't *get* an indemnity if it faces a particular risk related to the other party's actions. Subchapter 1 discusses a few of those risks.

1. Indemnity Obligation

Most indemnity clauses list the indemnified risks and provide some procedures for handling claims.

The provider should always promise to *indemnify* and *defend* against the claim. "Indemnify" means pay settlements or judgments, and "defend" means hire and pay attorneys to handle the case. Many indemnity clauses also give a *hold harmless* promise. That's not necessary because "hold harmless" generally means the same as "indemnify and defend," but it's common. See Subsection (b) in the following clause box.

The most common claim covered is an IP suit against the recipient, addressed in Subsection (a)(i) of the clause box.[33] But some indemnity clauses address suits about personal injuries or property damage. In Subsection (a)(ii) of the clause box, the concern is that, while providing services, the provider will drop a crate on someone's foot, or sexually harass someone, or compromise someone's private data, or burn down a building. The injured third party sues everyone, including the innocent recipient, who wants protection from the provider. Some providers accept these personal/property injury indemnities but limit their obligations to suits caused by negligence, rather than innocent mistakes, as in the example in the following clause box.

Usually, the indemnity promises protection from all covered claims, including stupid ones. If someone sues the recipient, even on a frivolous claim, the provider will pay the costs. That's how the example in the clause box works.

Often, indemnity clauses require that the recipient give the provider prompt notice of the claim and let the provider run the defense. And some clauses give the recipient authority to approve any settlement, or at least any settlement that restricts its rights. See Subsections (b) and (c) in the following clause box.

Many clauses also require that the provider defend both the recipient and its employees, officers, insurers, etc. Sometimes the promise to protect the recipient implies protection of these stakeholders, but as always, it never hurts to be clear. See the first

---

33. An IP indemnity covers the same ground as an IP warranty, so some of the same considerations apply. See Subchapter II.J.2.

The American Law Institute (ALI), a prestigious legal advisory body, has suggested that the law includes or should include an implied indemnity against IP infringement. This suggestion is controversial, but it's at least possible some sort of indemnity obligation will find its way into IT deals, even without the contract terms discussed previously. See ALI's *Principles of the Law of Software Contracts* (ALI 2010), § 3.01. And see footnote 30 in Subchapter II.J.4 ("Disclaimers of Warranty").

Indemnity

(a) *Indemnified Parties & Claims.* The "Indemnified Parties" are Recipient and its officers, directors, shareholders, parents, subsidiaries, agents, insurers, successors, and assigns. An "Indemnified Claim" is any third party claim, suit, or proceeding against the Indemnified Parties arising out of, related to, or alleging: (i) infringement of any patent, copyright, or other intellectual property right by the Software; or (ii) injury to or death of any individual, or any loss of or damage to real or tangible personal property, caused by the negligence of Provider or of any of its agents, subcontractors, or employees.

(b) *Indemnity.* Provider will indemnify, defend, and hold the Indemnified Parties harmless against any Indemnified Claim, provided Recipient gives Provider prompt notice of such Indemnified Claim. Provider's obligations set forth in the preceding sentence include, without limitation, retention and payment of attorneys and payment of court costs, as well as settlement at Provider's expense, payment of judgments, or both.

(c) *Litigation.* Provider will control the defense of any Indemnified Claim, including appeals, negotiations, and any settlement or compromise thereof; provided Recipient will have the right to approve the terms of any settlement or compromise that restricts its rights granted under this Agreement or subjects it to any ongoing obligations.

sentence of Subsection (a) in the clause box above. For distributors, this "Indemnified Parties" definition is particularly important. Does the provider have to indemnify the distributor's customers against IP suits, or just the distributor itself? Customers will almost certainly look to the distributor for protection, so without a promise from the provider, the distributor could find itself facing customers alone. Wherever possible, distributors should add "Distributor's licensees" or "end user customers" to the "Indemnified Parties" definition.

Note that the indemnity may do the recipient little good if it's restricted by the limitation of liability clause. The cost of a patent infringement suit, for example, usually far exceeds the demands permitted by a limitation of liability clause. So IT contracts often exempt the indemnity clause from the limitation of liability. See Subchapter II.L.4.

In some cases, the provider should consider asking the recipient for an indemnity, particularly where the recipient works in a risky field. Imagine the recipient hauls toxic chemicals, and the provider sells software that tracks the recipient's trucks. People injured in a chemical spill might sue both the recipient and any supplier remotely involved in managing the trucks, like the provider. So the provider might want to be on the *receiving end* of the personal injury indemnity in Subsection (a)(ii) of the clause box. Also, providers of online communications often ask for indemnities related to recipients' online misconduct. Such a provider might demand protection against "any claim, suit, or proceeding arising out of or related to Recipient's actual or alleged (1) infringement of third party intellectual property or privacy rights, (2) defamation of a third party, or (3) other breach of Provider's Acceptable Use Policy."[34]

Finally, software *distributors* sometimes indemnify their providers. Simply by doing business, the distributor creates all kinds of lawsuit risks. And the risks grow if the distributor makes wild claims in marketing materials or modifies the software or documentation in dangerous ways. An injured customer could easily drag the provider into a dispute with the distributor, even if the provider has no direct relationship with the customer. So the provider might demand protection against "any claim, suit, or proceeding by any customer of Distributor, except to the extent that such claim, suit, or proceeding arises out of or relates to: (a) alleged intellectual property infringement by the Software; (b) a failure of the Software to conform to its Specifications; or (c) an injury caused by the Software, excluding injuries caused by the Software's failure to perform as represented in Distributor's marketing materials but not in Provider's."

---

34. For acceptable use policies, see Appendix 5. The same appendix addresses the Digital Millennium Copyright Act, which helps protect online providers from recipients' copyright problems.

2. Exclusions from IP Indemnity

Providers often exclude certain intellectual property claims from their indemnity obligations. The point is to avoid covering claims the recipient brought on itself.

Obviously, the provider should try to avoid indemnity obligations for IP suits triggered by the recipient's breach of contract or by unauthorized software modification. And even if the provider itself performed the modification that caused the trouble, it should try to avoid an indemnity obligation if the recipient thought up the modification: if the recipient provided the specifications. Also, if the recipient refused a software update or upgrade that would have avoided the IP issue, it's arguably the recipient's own fault—and again the provider should try to avoid indemnity obligations. See Subsections (d)(i) through (d)(iv) in the following clause box.

Providers also try to avoid "interface" indemnities: responsibility for IP suits triggered by the software's use with some product the provider never anticipated. Imagine software that has no IP problems if used "normally." But the recipient does something *ab*normal. It hooks the software up to a device or application the provider never imagined—and *that* leads to an IP suit. From the provider's point of view, the suit is the recipient's problem.

Addressing the interface problem is tricky. Many providers' standard contracts simply state: "Provider will have no indemnity obligation related to use of the Software in combination with any third party hardware or software." The problem is, we always use software in combination with third party hardware and software: with computers, operating systems, word processing systems, reporting systems, communications systems, etc. Taken literally, the "no third party system" language means the indemnity only applies if the recipient leaves the software in the box. Of course, courts will avoid that sort of extreme interpretation, so that language creates a problem for both parties: uncertainty. No one knows what it means.

Subsection (d)(v) in the following clause box suggests a solution. If the provider's documentation or specifications[35] forbid use of the software with some device or application, the indemnity doesn't apply to interface with that product. And if the documentation or specs *recommend* a device or application, the indemnity does apply.

---

35. For documentation, see Chapter II.C. For specifications, see Chapter II.A.

Exclusions from IP Indemnity

(d) *Exclusions.* Provider's obligations set forth in Subsection __(b) above do not apply to the extent that an Indemnified Claim regarding intellectual property infringement arises out of:

(i) Recipient's violation of this Agreement;

(ii) revisions to the Software made without Provider's written consent;

(iii) Provider's modification of the Software in compliance with technical specifications provided by Recipient, or in compliance with a method or process provided by Recipient for implementing such specifications, unless Provider knew of the potential infringement at the time of such modification and did not notify Recipient;

(iv) Recipient's failure to incorporate Software updates or upgrades that would have avoided the alleged infringement, provided Provider offered such updates or upgrades without fees or charges not otherwise required pursuant to this Agreement;

(v) use of the Software in combination with hardware or software not provided by Provider: (A) that is specifically forbidden by the Documentation or Specifications; or (B) that is not designated in the Documentation or Specifications as available for interface with the Software, unless such hardware or software is necessary for the Software to perform a function listed in the Documentation or Specifications.

For instance, the documentation might read: "Now generate a report in Microsoft Excel." That extends the indemnity to IP suits triggered by interface with Excel. Finally, if the specs and documentation don't mention the third party product, the indemnity applies if interface with that product is necessary for use of this software: for it to function as described in the specs.

The language of your interface clause depends on your software. It may be hard to say what interfaces are "necessary" for system operations. Where you can't, the recipient might favor an indemnity for interface with systems that "contribute" to performance of one of the functions listed in the specs. The provider, on the other hand, might want to eliminate the "necessary" concept altogether and simply indemnify for interface with products listed and not forbidden in the documentation. Obviously, the recipient should push for a broad definition of indemnified claims, while the provider should push for a narrow one.

L. Limitation of Liability

Limitation of liability clauses appear in almost all software and services contracts. They usually protect the provider, but sometimes they protect both parties—particularly in distribution agreements.

To newcomers, limitation of liability often seems bizarre. The clause says that if one party injures the other, it's not responsible for the full damages. Imagine the provider supplies defective software. The software malfunctions, and as a result, the recipient loses a million dollars. Imagine also that the limitation of liability clause caps the provider's liability at $50,000. The result: the provider is liable for *one twentieth* of the recipient's loss. Even if everyone agrees the malfunction was the provider's fault, the provider owes $50K, and that's all.

What recipient would agree to such a thing, and why? The answer is, *almost every recipient*, and there's a good reason why.

The feature of the IT industry that makes it so profitable makes limitation of liability standard. That feature is *scalability*. Information technology is an unusually scalable tool: it can be used to achieve goals geometrically more valuable than the tool itself. You can use a five-thousand-dollar software program to design a half-billion-dollar bridge. You can use a ten-thousand-dollar computer to manage a billion-dollar asset portfolio. And that same low-cost software application or computer can single-handedly *ruin* a half-billion-dollar bridge or a billion-dollar asset portfolio.

If the provider faced potential liability of a billion dollars, or even a half-million dollars, with every $5,000 sale, it couldn't do business. One malfunction could wipe out ten years of profits, or the whole company. That's why software and IT services providers insist on limitations of liability.

Still, limitations of liability can be a bit hard to swallow. In fact, courts often won't enforce the clause if they think the recipient didn't grasp its importance, particularly if the recipient is a consumer. That's why the limitation of liability usually stands out, printed in capital letters (like the examples in the clause boxes below). The provider wants to establish that if the recipient didn't notice the clause, or recognize its importance, it's the recipient's own fault. Providers should take other precautions to increase their chances of enforcement, addressed in Subchapter 3, page 111.

Limitation of liability clauses come in two common flavors: dollar caps and exclusions of consequential damages. Most contracts feature both, as overlapping protections. Many clauses also have exceptions: types of liability that are *not* limited. We'll address each of these in turn.

Finally, note that some software and services contracts limit the recipient's liability too. The usual recipient rationale is: "If your liability's limited, so is ours." The examples in the following clause boxes protect only the provider, but you can easily make them two-way clauses. For instance, instead of "Provider's liability will not exceed . . . ," your contract would say: "Neither party's liability will exceed . . ." Providers should be aware, however, that two-way clauses create some special risks for them. See Subchapter 4, page 112.

1. Dollar Cap

The simplest part of the limitation of liability clause caps the parties' liability at a dollar figure.

Dollar Cap Limitation of Liability

PROVIDER'S LIABILITY ARISING OUT OF OR RELATED TO THIS AGREEMENT WILL NOT EXCEED $_____.

• • • •

PROVIDER'S LIABILITY ARISING OUT OF OR RELATED TO THIS AGREEMENT WILL NOT EXCEED THE ANNUAL LICENSE FEE.

The dollar cap could be a million or five thousand or anything else. Often the figure isn't set ahead of time. Instead, it's calculated through some formula, as in the second example in the previous clause box.

Providers should avoid an excessively low dollar cap, as explained in Subchapter 3, page 111. But otherwise, the cap is arbitrary. You can pick almost any figure or any way of calculating a figure. Providers often forget this and complain that a high dollar cap isn't "fair." The size of the dollar cap depends on leverage, not fairness. In other words, which party wants the deal most, and what risks can the parties accept?

2. *Exclusion of Consequential Damages*

The exclusion of consequential damages focuses on the *type* of liability, not the dollar amount. The clause may exclude "indirect," "special," "punitive," and various other types of damages. All of those but *punitive*—discussed in the following—are flavors of consequential damages.

To understand consequential damages, let's return to our example of a software application used to design a half-billion-dollar bridge. The software malfunctions, and as a result, the bridge is defective and falls apart. The recipient designed the bridge and owns it, and it wants two kinds of compensation from the provider: direct and consequential damages. The *direct* damage is compensation for the type of losses usually caused by software failures. Half-billion-dollar bridge design isn't the norm for that application (or any, arguably), so direct damages probably wouldn't cover the cost of the bridge. They might cover the cost of a much smaller defective product, and the cost of replacing the software. The *consequential* damage is the price tag on all the unique consequences of *this* particular failure. That would cover the bridge, as well as the cost of paying off any injured drivers or pedestrians, loss of the recipient's time, loss of other business opportunities, loss of reputation, etc.[36]

In other words, consequential damages are unpredictable and theoretically unlimited (though some state laws impose limits). That's why software and services vendors generally insist on limiting them.

---

36. The line between direct and consequential damages depends on the context, and it's not always clear. Direct damages can run high.

Exclusion of Consequential Damages

IN NO EVENT WILL PROVIDER BE LIABLE TO RECIPIENT FOR ANY CONSEQUENTIAL, INDIRECT, SPECIAL, INCIDENTAL, OR PUNITIVE DAMAGES ARISING OUT OF OR RELATED TO THIS AGREEMENT.

Obviously, a dollar cap would also prevent liability for much of the money at stake in a consequential damages claim. The two clauses overlap.

Finally, limitation of liability clauses sometimes exclude punitive damages. Punitive damages go beyond compensation and punish someone who's done wrong. They're usually not available in contract cases. But the law isn't always predictable, and there's no harm in throwing "punitive" into the list with "consequential," "special," etc., as in the example above.

3. Unconscionability and Required Clarifications

In theory, a limitation of liability is perfectly enforceable. Still, courts often look for a way out if the clause seems unfair in the extreme—particularly if the recipient is a consumer. Courts will set aside the clause if it's "unconscionable" or "opposed to public policy."[37] It's hard to define "unconscionability," so it's hard to give clear instructions on avoiding it. If you're the provider, use the following two questions to help avoid unconscionability. First, is the clause drafted to avoid any meaningful liability for your own wrongdoing? If so, you may have a problem. Second, would a sane recipient sign the contract after reading the clause? If not—if you're hoping recipients just won't notice the limitation of liability—you probably do have a problem.

You can reduce the chances of unconscionability through a few disclaimers and clarifications.

Most courts won't enforce a limitation of negligence liability unless it's explicit, so negligence should appear in the clause, as in Subsection (i) in the following example. The provider should also list

---

37. Some would argue, for instance, that courts should never enforce an exclusion of consequential damages for personal injuries caused by consumer software.

Clarifications and Disclaimers

THE LIABILITIES LIMITED BY THIS SECTION __ APPLY: (i) TO LIABILITY FOR NEGLIGENCE; (ii) REGARDLESS OF THE FORM OF ACTION, WHETHER IN CONTRACT, TORT, STRICT PRODUCT LIABILITY, OR OTHERWISE; (iii) EVEN IF PROVIDER IS ADVISED IN ADVANCE OF THE POSSIBILITY OF THE DAMAGES IN QUESTION AND EVEN IF SUCH DAMAGES WERE FORESEEABLE; AND (iv) EVEN IF RECIPIENT'S REMEDIES FAIL OF THEIR ESSENTIAL PURPOSE. If applicable law limits the application of the provisions of this Section __, Provider's liability will be limited to the maximum extent permissible.

---

just about every form of action the parties are likely to address, so there can be no doubt about the intended reach of the clause, as in Subsection (ii).

Courts sometimes refuse to enforce the limitation of liability because the provider had warning of the loss in question, or the loss was foreseeable. Subsection (iii) in the clause box addresses that risk. Courts also sometimes refuse enforcement where the clause leaves the recipient no meaningful remedy. The best solution is to allow a meaningful remedy, as suggested above, but the provider can also have the recipient agree that no remedy is required. That's why Subsection (iv) in the clause box says the clause survives even if the recipient's remedies "fail of their essential purpose."

Finally, the provider should think about salvaging something from the limitation of liability clause even if all these precautions fail: even if a court refuses to enforce the clause. The last sentence in the clause box gives courts instructions on paring back an unconscionable or otherwise enforceable clause, without eliminating it.

4. Exceptions: Liability That's Not Limited

The parties often agree that the clause won't limit certain forms of liability.

Generally, these exceptions carve out liabilities created by the contract itself. The most common exceptions are for indemnity and liqui-

> ## Exceptions to Limitation of Liability
>
> This Section __ does not apply to: (i) claims pursuant to any provision of this Agreement calling for liquidated damages; (ii) claims pursuant to Section __ (*Indemnity*); or (iii) claims for attorneys' fees and other litigation costs Recipient becomes entitled to recover as a prevailing party in any action.
>
> • • • •
>
> The limitations of liability in this Section __ do not apply to: (i) Recipient's obligation to pay fees pursuant to Section __ (*License and Service Fees*); or (ii) any claims against Recipient for infringement of Provider's intellectual property, including without limitation copyrights in the Software.

dated damages—both addressed in the first example in the clause box above.[38] The indemnity exception is particularly important and particularly contentious in many deals. If the limitation of liability restricts the provider's IP indemnity obligations, those obligations could be almost meaningless, since the cost of a patent suit could be millions more than the limitation of liability allows. Providers, however, often refuse to exclude indemnity from the limitation of liability. A compromise clause might read: "The Provisions Subsections 10(a)(i) (*Dollar Cap*) and 10(a)(ii) (*Exclusion of Consequential Damages*) do not apply to liability pursuant to Subsection 9(b) (*IP Indemnity*). PROVIDER'S LIABILITY ARISING OUT OF OR RELATED TO SUBSECTION 9(b) WILL NOT EXCEED 5 TIMES THE ANNUAL LICENSE FEE."

In a two-way limitation of liability clause—protecting the recipient as well as the provider—providers should consider some additional exceptions. The first has to do with intellectual property infringement. What if the recipient infringes the provider's copyright by creating too many copies of the software? What if, instead of creating two copies, as authorized in the license section, the recipient

---

38. For indemnity and liquidated damages, see Chapters II.K and II.Q. Recipients should avoid provisions that exclude the provider's obligation to *indemnify* the recipient but not its obligation to *defend* the recipient. As Chapter II.K explains, both are crucial. That's why the first example in the clause box above references the entire indemnity section, which usually includes both.

creates a thousand? If the limitation of liability clause caps damages at the contract price, the recipient arguably gets a thousand for the price of two. Of course, a court might not stand for such contract-assisted theft, but the provider shouldn't take the risk. That's why the second example in the previous clause box carves out liability for IP infringement by the recipient.

Second, the provider should be certain the clause can't be interpreted as a guarantee that the recipient won't have to pay anything other than license fees, even if it breaches the contract. What if the recipient breaches the contract in two ways: by failing to pay a year's worth of fees, and in some other way, like failing to observe nondisclosure requirements? If the dollar cap limits each party's liability to one year's worth of fees, the recipient could argue that it's only liability is for the unpaid fees. It could breach the contract's other terms with impunity, thanks to the dollar cap. At least, the contract could be interpreted that way. So the provider should protect itself by clarifying that the liability for fees stands outside the clause (or at least outside the dollar cap). See the second example in the previous clause box.

Providers granting mutual clauses should peruse the contract for other liabilities that should *not* be limited. Is there some recipient promise that, if broken, would trigger large consequential damages, or otherwise lead to losses higher than the cap? Breach of a government restricted rights clause might cost the provider a fortune, for instance. So the provider might want terms saying: "The limitations of liability of this Section 8 do not apply to breach of the provisions of Subsection 14(d) (*Government Restricted Rights*)."[39] In general, providers should consider the limitation of liability clause *their* shield. If the protection shields the recipient too, the provider should think through the risks and create exceptions for any it can't accept.

M. Use of Trademarks

A trademark license is like a software copyright license. It authorizes use of trademarks without transferring ownership. Businesses use these licenses to facilitate marketing.

You don't need a trademark license if one party just wants to issue a press release talking about its relationship with the other. But if a party wants to make extensive marketing use of the other party's

---

39. See Chapter III.G.

Use of Names and Trademarks

Recipient hereby grants Provider a license to include Recipient's primary logo, illustrated on Attachment __ (the "Logo"), in any customer list or press release announcing this Agreement, provided Provider first submits each such press release or customer list to Recipient and receives written approval, which approval will not unreasonably be withheld. Goodwill associated with the Logo inures solely to Recipient, and Provider will take no action to damage the goodwill associated with the Logo or with Recipient.

• • • •

Provider hereby grants Distributor a license to reproduce its trademarks listed on Attachment __ on marketing and advertising materials and packaging related to any Product (collectively, "Advertisements"); provided (a) the Product conforms to the quality requirements listed in Attachment __ and (b) Distributor observes Provider's standard guidelines on trademark usage, attached hereto as Attachment __, including any written amendment provided by Provider in its sole discretion. All goodwill associated with such trademarks inures solely to Provider, and Distributor will take no action to damage the goodwill associated with the Trademarks or with Provider. In the event that Provider notifies Distributor in writing that any Product or Advertisement (pending or published) does not conform to the requirements of this Section __, Distributor will promptly withdraw it or remove all Provider trademarks; provided that Provider will not unreasonably issue such notice.

name, it needs a trademark license (assuming the name is a trademark). Such "extensive" use would include putting the name on product packages, for instance, in a distribution relationship.[40] And use of logos almost always requires a license.

The trademark owner should supervise use of its marks. It should review press releases, customer lists, and other marketing

---

40. It's hard to define "extensive." If in doubt, get a license—or talk to an experienced attorney.

documents to make sure they're consistent with its public image. And in a distribution agreement, the trademark owner should check on the quality of any product sold using its trademarks. This type of supervision doesn't just make good business sense; it's necessary to preserve trademark rights. Trademarks are like friends: if you don't treat them well, you lose them. A *naked license*—a grant of trademark rights without supervision—can invalidate the trademark.

Both examples in the previous clause box help avoid naked licensing by granting supervision rights. In the first example, the trademark owner has to approve trademark usage in advance. That's the best system for the owner, but it's not always practical, particularly where the other party issues hundreds of ads. So the second example does away with advance approval. Instead, it requires that the other party observe the owner's trademark usage guidelines. And if the owner does notice misuse of its mark, the other party has to withdraw the offending ad. The second example also addresses the quality of the underlying product—promising the owner that its trademark won't be associated with shoddy merchandise.

But contract language might not do the trick alone. To preserve trademark status, the owner should *actually supervise* use of its marks.

On a related note, the trademark licensee should agree not to damage the owner's goodwill, as in both examples in the previous clause box. "Goodwill" is the value behind trademarks: the reputation for quality associated with products and services sold under the mark. Of course, the licensee more or less agrees to preserve goodwill by agreeing to obey the owner's trademark policies and rules. But the more general promise adds to the owner's protection.

Finally, trademark owners should usually ensure that goodwill "inures to" the owner, as in both examples in the previous clause box. In other words, the owner gets the legal benefit goodwill, even though the other party may be creating some of that goodwill through its use of the trademark.

N. Training

Training clauses are most common in software licenses, though they may appear in any sale of software or systems. In these clauses, the provider promises to help the recipient learn how to operate a computer system.

Training

Provider will provide training courses on operation of the Licensed Product, at Recipient's _____ facility, at such times during business hours as Recipient may reasonably request. Each training course will last ___ hours. Recipient may enroll up to ___ of its staff members in any training course, and Provider will provide a hard copy of the Licensed Product's standard training manual for each enrollee. Each training course will be taught by a technician with no fewer than ___ years' full-time experience operating _____ software systems. Provider will provide the first ___ trainings without additional charge and will provide additional trainings at its standard rates.

• • • •

Without additional charge, Provider will provide such training on use of the Software as Recipient may reasonably request, and the parties will negotiate in good faith regarding the time and place of such training.

Some clauses provide significant detail about training parameters: duration and size of courses, expertise of instructors, cost (if any), etc.—as in the first example in the clause box above. But some training clauses leave the details out, on the assumption that the parties can work them out later.

Training is a professional service. So if training forms a major part of the transaction, review Chapter I.E.

O. Non-Compete and Non-Solicitation

A non-compete clause provides that one party won't poach the other's customers or otherwise compete for the other's business. A non-solicitation clause forbids any attempt to hire away employees. Both clauses are common in professional services contracts.

Non-compete and non-solicitation clauses also appear in many employment contracts. The employee promises not to compete with the employer during or after employment, and not to lure other employees away. This book doesn't directly address employment contracts, though some of the principles in this chapter do apply. You should handle employment contracts with care. Employment law has its own set of restrictions, particularly related to non-compete clauses.

This chapter looks at non-compete clauses first, then at non-solicitation.

1. Non-Compete

Usually, a non-compete clause binds the provider, rather than the recipient, though both are possible. As a result of providing services, the provider gains information or connections that could help it compete with the recipient. The recipient finds creation of a well-armed competitor too high a price to pay for the services, so the parties agree that the provider won't use its new resources to compete, or won't compete at all.

Non-compete clauses butt heads with public policies favoring competition and protecting everyone's right to make a living. So an overly restrictive clause may be unenforceable.[41] In fact, in at least one state, California, non-competes are entirely unenforceable against individuals (except in the sale of a business or dissolution of a partnership),[42] and you could theoretically face liability for trying to prevent competition. So before drafting a non-compete, you should consider consulting a lawyer with experience for your state. In general, though, three principles should guide your thinking on non-compete clauses. First, you're more likely to enforce a non-compete clause against a company than an individual. (And the fact that a freelance provider incorporates or refers to himself as "Ernie's Software Company" probably won't push him into the company column.) Second, you shouldn't include a non-compete clause unless there's a reason this particular deal needs one. Would performance of services give the provider access to information, contacts, or other resources that could help it compete? That's a good reason for a non-compete clause. The recipient's general paranoia isn't. Third, don't try to close off a substantial part of the provider's future business. Make sure the non-compete clause leaves the provider room to make a good living, or to operate a good business.

---

41. Most contracts should include a severability clause, providing that one unenforceable term won't doom the whole agreement. See Chapter III.K.

42. See California Business & Professions Code § 16600 *et seq.*

No Competition

During the term of this Agreement and for ___ months after termination, Provider will not solicit or provide services to any customer or potential customer of Recipient identified to Provider in writing during the term of this Agreement, provided such writing is transmitted as a necessary step in facilitating the provision of services or payments required by this Agreement. The provisions of the preceding sentence do not apply to customers or potential customers Provider identified before the Effective Date.

• • • •

During the term of this Agreement and for ___ years following termination, Provider will not solicit or accept employment, including without limitation as an independent contractor, from any Customer (as defined in the next sentence). A "Customer" is: (a) any person or entity that purchased goods or services from Recipient during the term of this Agreement or during the ___ months preceding the Effective Date; and (b) any person or entity Recipient identified as a potential purchaser of its goods or services in any document disclosed to Provider during the term of this Agreement. Provider will pay Recipient ___ % of any payments received from any Customer for products or services provided in breach of this Section ___, as liquidated damages.

• • • •

During the term of this Agreement and for the ___ months following termination, Provider will not accept employment from, work for, provide services to, set up, serve as a sole proprietor or partner or other stakeholder in, or operate any Competitor (as defined in the next sentence), or own more than 1% of the outstanding shares or securities representing the right to vote for the election of directors or other managing authority of any Competitor. A "Competitor" is any person or entity that provides _____ *[list products and/or services]* in _____ *[list geographic territory]*. In the event of breach of the provisions of this Section ___, Provider will pay Recipient the sum of $_____ as liquidated damages.

A non-compete clause can address direct competition, indirect competition, or both. Direct competition involves selling to the recipient's customers or participating in a business that offers the same products or services. Recipients worry about direct competition when the provider works in the same field, or could. For instance, both parties could provide computer programming. All three examples in the previous clause box address direct competition.

Indirect competition involves provision of services to competitors, not actual competition. The provider may offer computer system design, while the recipient sells shoes. But the recipient doesn't want the provider using knowledge of the recipient's systems to build systems for rival shoe shops. The third example in the clause box addresses indirect competition.

The first example in the clause box provides a narrow definition of competition—a definition favored by providers. The provider agrees not to use the recipient's customer lists to seek new clients. It can compete in other ways. And the customer lists in question must have been disclosed during the parties' collaboration. The clause doesn't prevent sales to customers the provider discovered through some other source, or to the recipient's customers, if the provider can prove it identified them before the contract. Finally, the recipient must have disclosed the customer lists for legitimate purposes: to facilitate provision of services. It can't just e-mail its entire list of customers, to restrict the provider.

The second two examples in the clause box provide broader definitions of competition, more often favored by recipients. In the second example, the provider can't sell to any customer of the recipient or any potential customer identified during the term of the contract. And in the third example, the recipient can't sell services to a competing business, or run such a business.

Obviously, providers shouldn't accept a clause that too narrowly restricts them. And as noted previously, recipients shouldn't ask for such a clause, to preserve enforceability. Various provisions address these issues by limiting the reach of non-compete clauses. All three previous examples have a time limitation. The prohibition ends after some period of months or years. And the third example has a geographic limitation. You can also limit the clause by *naming* the competitors that worry the recipient: "During the term of this Agreement and for eighteen (18) months thereafter, Provider will sell no products or services to SiblingRival LLP, Leading Brand Solutions, Inc., or Nemesis Corporation."

Finally, some non-compete clauses provide for liquidated damages, as in the second two examples in the clause box on page 119. It's usually hard to determine the size of the recipient's injury if the provider breaches the clause. So the liquidated damages provision fixes a damages amount. The amount may be a percentage of the provider's revenues from a stolen customer, as in the second example, or a fixed fee, as in the third example. The key requirement is that the amount bear *some* relation to the recipient's likely losses. If you include liquidated damages, review Chapter II.Q.

The non-compete clause isn't the law's only tool for protecting customer lists and other competition-related information. Those items might be trade secrets. A detailed explanation of trade secrets lies outside the scope of this book. But in most states, a trade secret is information that is: (a) valuable because it's not widely known or easily discovered by people who could use it; and (b) subject to reasonable efforts to maintain secrecy.[43] Trade secret infringement is against the law even without a non-compete clause.

2. Non-Solicitation

Non-solicitation clauses can restrict either the provider or the recipient. They make sure professional services relationships don't turn into employee-poaching expeditions. As a result of close contact, one party might identify valuable members of the other's staff.

Of course, solicitation can be difficult to prove. What if the one party slyly hints to the other's employees that better opportunities might be available elsewhere? What if a party offers a job but then claims the employee started the conversation? Some contracts address this by going beyond non-solicitation to forbid *hiring*: "During the term of this Agreement and for 12 months thereafter, Recipient will not hire, as an employee or independent contractor, any person employed by Provider during the term of this Agreement." A clause like that, however, might offend the very employees you're trying to keep, and it might not be enforceable. If you want an antihiring clause, talk to a lawyer with experience for your state.

---

43. This definition paraphrases the Uniform Trade Secrets Act, adopted in most states.

> ## No Solicitation of Employees
>
> During the term of this Agreement and for ___ months after termination, neither party will directly or indirectly solicit any of the other's employees to consider alternate employment.

Non-solicitation clauses can address independent contractors as well as employees. "During the term of this Agreement and for 18 months thereafter, Provider will not directly or indirectly offer employment (as a contractor or employee) to any independent contractor who provides technology support services to Recipient during the term of this Agreement." In drafting a contractor clause, remember that every nonemployee who provides services counts as an independent contractor. Do you really want to keep the other party from retaining your accountant, or your plumber, janitor, or phone company? Specify the type of contractor you mean.

P. Software Audits

An audit clause helps the provider protect against unauthorized copying and use of software. Audit terms are appropriate for end user licenses and distribution agreements.

An audit clause authorizes the provider to review the recipient's books and computers. The provider searches for evidence of copies in excess of the license, use beyond the scope authorized, or distribution without royalty payments.

> ## Software Audit
>
> Provider may audit Recipient's use of the Licensed Product on ___ days' advance written notice. Recipient will cooperate with the audit, including by providing access to any books, computers, records, or other information that relate or may relate to use of the Licensed Product. Such audit will not unreasonably interfere with Recipient's business activities. In the event that an

> audit reveals unauthorized use, reproduction, distribution, or other exploitation of the Licensed Product, Recipient will reimburse Provider for the reasonable cost of the audit, in addition to such other rights and remedies as Provider may have. Provider will not conduct an audit more than once per _____.

Audits can be a source of terror for recipients, because the law provides some high fees for copyright infringement.

Q. Liquidated Damages

When one party breaches a contract, the other generally has a right to damages: to money that compensates for any injuries. But in some relationships, the parties know in advance that damages will be hard to calculate. So they specify the amount the breaching party will have to pay, in a liquidated damages clause.

Imagine the recipient wants customized software to improve its efficiency, and the provider agrees to write it within four months. If the provider delivers late or not at all, the recipient will have wasted a lot of time. It will also have missed out on savings and business opportunities. But it's hard to put a dollar figure on lost time or improvements brought by an untried system. So the parties agree in advance on *liquidated* damages. The provider will pay $150 for every day of delay and $25,000 if it never delivers the software at all. This liquidated damages pact should help prevent disputes about the consequences of delay. And if the parties do go to court, the clause should prevent an expensive dispute about damages.

Don't confuse liquidated damages with early termination fees. As explained in Subchapter II.T.3 ("Termination for Convenience"), some contracts let a party terminate early in exchange for a fee. This termination for convenience is not a breach of contract. It's authorized. So the fee isn't a damages calculation. It's the contract *price* for early termination. Liquidated damages, on the other hand, are *damages for breach* of contract.

Courts will only enforce a liquidated damages clause if it meets two conditions. First, at the time the parties sign the contract, likely damages have to be uncertain or difficult to prove. Second, the

---

Specification of Liquidated Damages

Provider will credit Recipient __ % of the License Fee, as liquidated damages, for each business day between the Due Date and any later date Provider delivers the Software; provided such liquidated damages will not exceed __ % of the License Fee. Such liquidated damages are Recipient's exclusive remedy for late delivery but they do not preclude other remedies for other injuries.

• • • •

In the event that Recipient materially breaches this Agreement and Provider terminates on that basis, Recipient will pay Provider, as liquidated damages, __ % of the Service Fees not yet invoiced. The provisions of the preceding sentence do not limit Recipient's obligation to pay Service Fees already invoiced.

• • • •

In the event that the System does not provide the functionality listed in Item __ of the Technical Specifications, Provider will pay Recipient $_____, as liquidated damages. Such liquidated damages are Recipient's exclusive remedy for such breach, but they do not preclude other remedies for other injuries.

---

damages have to serve as compensation for injuries, not as a penalty. Penalty clauses are unenforceable. So the liquidated damages amount should roughly approximate the injured party's projected losses. Of course, you don't know how much the injured party would lose if the other party breached. But you can at least guess at a range and fix the liquidated damages somewhere in that range. It doesn't matter if you guess wrong. What matters is that, at the point of executing the contract, the guess was reasonable. If the parties just pick some high number, with little or no relationship to likely losses, a court will probably consider it a penalty.

A liquidated damages clause should have two parts: a specification of damages and a justification.

The parties can set a specific dollar amount as liquidated damages, as in the last example in the clause box above. Or they can provide a formula for calculation of damages, as in the first two examples.

> ### *Justification for Liquidated Damages*
>
> The parties agree that the damages set forth in this Section __ are liquidated damages and not penalties and that they are reasonable in light of the harm that will be caused by breach, the difficulties of proof of loss, and the inconvenience and infeasibility of otherwise obtaining an adequate remedy.

Liquidated damages are generally exclusive: the injured party can't get any other compensation for the injury in question. It's often a good idea to clarify that the clause doesn't rule out additional damages for *other* injuries, as in the first and last examples in the clause box on the preceding page. Some contracts, however, provide that liquidated damages are not the only remedy available, even for the injury in question. "This Section 7 does not preclude the injured party from seeking compensation for actual damages." In many states, a provision like that would render the whole liquidated damages clause unenforceable.

The justification part of the clause addresses the requirements for liquidated damages. The parties agree that the liquidated damages are necessary because figuring actual losses would be so hard. They also agree that they didn't intend the clause as a penalty and that they used an estimate of actual losses to set the liquidated damages amount. See the clause box above.

The fact that the parties state these justification claims doesn't make them so. A court will make its own assessment. But neither party should be able to argue that it didn't understand the clause's purpose.

R. Financial and System Stability

When one company comes to rely on another, it often wants assurances of the other's financial stability, and of the stability of its vital IT systems. Technology companies address this in a variety of ways, particularly through reporting clauses and insurance clauses. These stability clauses crop up most often in services agreement, where the recipient wants assurances of the provider's stability. That's the case with the following examples, but there's no reason the provider can't request stability assurances from the recipient.

1. *Financial and Technical Reporting*

Reporting clauses give the recipient early warning of trouble. If the provider faces financial trouble, it could tumble into bankruptcy, and it could lose the will or the ability to perform vital services, like keeping sensitive data safe. If the recipient sees trouble far enough in advance, it might be able to protect itself—by terminating the contract, retaining another vendor, taking back the data, asserting legal claims, etc.

The first example in the clause box below calls on the provider to perform a "SAS-70" audit. That stands for "Statement on Auditing Standards 70," and it refers to an auditing standard maintained by the American Institute of Certified Public Accountants (AICPA). As the AICPA puts it, a SAS-70 is a "Report on the Processing of Transactions by Service Organizations." An accounting firm reviews the internal controls on the provider's transaction processing systems, including the security of its IT infrastructure. In a "Type II" report,

---

Reporting Clauses

No less than once per _____, Provider will retain a certified public accounting firm to perform a SAS-70 audit and to produce a SAS-70 Type II report. Provider will provide such report to Recipient promptly after receipt thereof, and such report will be considered Confidential Information disclosed by Provider pursuant to Section __ (*Nondisclosure*) of this Agreement.

• • • •

Once per _____, on reasonable advance notice, Recipient may review Provider's financial books and records, including a current balance sheet, a statement of income and losses for the preceding 12 months, and a statement of cash flow for such 12 months. Such review will be conducted in Provider's facility, and Recipient will have no right to retain copies of any books and records. All books and records and all information contained therein will be considered Confidential Information disclosed by Provider pursuant to Section __ (*Nondisclosure*).

the auditor describes the systems and offers an opinion on their effectiveness. A "Type I" report lacks the opinion, so tech recipients generally choose Type II—though plenty of contracts fail to specify the type.

The second example in the clause box gives the recipient the right to review the provider's key books and records. Obviously, providers should hesitate before granting anyone that kind of access. The clause makes the most sense when the provider is a small company without a track record of stability, and a valuable customer plans to rely on it for vital services. (The clause wouldn't make sense for a publicly traded provider, which discloses its financial performance to the public every quarter.)

Note that in both clauses, the provider's reports and records are "Confidential Information" pursuant to the contract's nondisclosure clause. If the contract lacks such a clause, the provider should consider adding one or signing a separate nondisclosure agreement.[44]

2. *Insurance*

An insurance clause requires that the provider maintain various insurance policies. That helps ensure that money will be available to compensate the recipient for damages the provider causes.

The example in the following clause box calls for a relatively broad spectrum of insurance policies. But some contracts add another type of coverage: insurance for damage caused by technology-related errors and omissions. And many IT contracts require less, limiting themselves to "commercial general liability insurance" (covered in Subsection (a)).

The clauses' policy limits (two million, five million, etc.) vary with the parties' needs. The same goes for the minimum financial rating of the insurance carriers, as well as the source of that rating. Many clauses call for "insurance with carriers rated A- or better by A.M. Best Company."[45]

The coverage period varies too. Some contracts call for insurance during the term of the agreement and no longer. But if claims impacting the recipient could come in after contract termination,

---

44. See Chapter II.H.
45. Standard & Poor's and Moody's appear in many of these clauses too.

Insurance

During the term of this Agreement and for _____ thereafter, Provider will maintain in full force and effect: (a) commercial general liability insurance covering personal injury and property damage, including without limitation contractual liability, with limits of at least $_____ per occurrence and $_____ in the aggregate; (b) business automobile liability insurance for all vehicles, including those owned or rented by Provider or its employees, covering personal injury and property damage, with a limit of at least $_____ per occurrence; and (c) worker's compensation and employer's liability insurance, with limits of at least $_____. Provider will maintain all such insurance with carriers rated __ or better by _____. The insurance policies required pursuant to this Section __ will stipulate that they are primary insurance and that no insurance policy or self-insurance program of Recipient will be called upon to contribute. Before commencement of Services, and from time to time thereafter upon renewal of any such policy of insurance, Provider will provide Recipient with certificates of insurance evidencing the above coverages and naming Recipient as certificate holder entitled to 30 days' written notice following any cancellation, reduction, or change in coverage.

---

the clause should require that insurance coverage continue for some set period, as in the first sentence of the example in the clause box.

S. Alternate Dispute Resolution

Alternate dispute resolution clauses aim to keep the parties out of court. They provide alternative procedures for resolving arguments.

The following clause box provides three alternate dispute resolution (ADR) clauses: escalation, mediation, and arbitration. Your contract might include any or all of these.

Escalation is the least formal alternate dispute resolution procedure. It calls on the parties to bump the argument up to senior

Dispute Resolution

In the event of dispute, either party may call for escalation by written notice to the other. Within __ business days of such notice, each party will designate an executive with authority to make commitments that would resolve the dispute (a "Senior Manager"). The parties' Senior Managers will meet in person or by telephone ("Dispute Conference") within __ business days of their designation and will negotiate in good faith to resolve the dispute. Except to the extent necessary to prevent irreparable harm or to preserve rights or remedies, neither party will initiate arbitration or litigation until __ days after the Dispute Conference.

• • • •

If the parties cannot themselves resolve a dispute arising out of or related to this Agreement, they will attempt to resolve such dispute through mediation under the auspices of _____ [ADR association], in _____ [city], with the parties sharing equally the costs of mediation. Except to the extent necessary to prevent irreparable harm or to preserve rights or remedies, neither party will initiate arbitration or litigation until __ days after the first mediation conference, unless the other party has materially breached its obligations set forth in the preceding sentence.

• • • •

Any claim arising out of or related to this Agreement, including without limitation claims related to the parties' negotiations and inducements to enter into this Agreement, will be submitted to mandatory, binding arbitration under the auspices of _____ (the "ADR Association"), in _____ [city], with the parties sharing equally the costs of arbitration. Arbitration will proceed according to the standard _____ rules of the ADR Association. This Section __ does not limit either party's right to provisional or ancillary remedies from a court of competent jurisdiction before, after, or during the pendency of any arbitration, and the exercise of any such remedy does not waive either party's right to arbitration. Judgment on an arbitration award may be entered by any court with competent jurisdiction.

executives, as in the first example in the previous clause box. An escalation clause should provide that no one can file a lawsuit until the senior executives have met and tried to resolve the dispute.

Mediation is the next step. In a mediation clause, like the second example in the clause box, the parties agree to work with a third party who can help resolve the dispute. The mediator tries to broker a deal, including by helping each party see the disadvantages of litigating.

Arbitration is the most common ADR clause in IT contracts. In provisions like the third example in the clause box, the parties agree to let a third party *decide* their dispute. This third party arbitrator acts like a judge. Usually, the contract provides that arbitration is "mandatory and binding." "Mandatory" means that if one party wants to arbitrate, the other can't escape and go to court. And "binding" means the arbitrator's decision is final. There's no appeal to a court or anyone else (unless the arbitrator abuses his or her discretion—does something clearly improper, like accepting a bribe or ignoring the obvious legal rules governing the case). In other words, arbitration creates a private "people's court,"[46] with power to act like a real government court.

Your ADR clause can name the mediator or arbitrator—the "neutral"—in advance, or it can authorize the parties to pick one or more neutrals. Three-person panels are common for arbitration: "Each party will select an arbitrator who has no financial or family relationship with such party and identify him or her in writing within 10 days of the demand for arbitration. The two arbitrators will select a third arbitrator within 10 days of written identification of both." (Three-person panels cost more, but with more arbitrators, you have less chance of error, bias, or random craziness.)

Members of the IT industry often find mediators and arbitrators through dispute resolution companies, like the American Arbitration Association or JAMS.[47] Those companies usually hire lawyers and retired judges, though in some cases they bring in specialists with

---

46. In fact, most TV court shows are really arbitrations. The TV "judge" is an arbitrator. He or she has the power to resolve the dispute because the parties have signed an arbitration agreement.

47. JAMS originally stood for "Judicial Arbitration and Mediation Service," but now the company's name is just "JAMS."

appropriate technical expertise. Some trade groups and community organizations offer ADR services too—sometimes for little or no money—so you might consider designating one of those. Many ADR companies and organizations provide language for mediation and arbitration clauses, so check to see if your chosen association has language you might prefer to the examples in the previous clause box.

ADR associations may provide their own private rules of civil procedure: rules for conducting discovery and otherwise running an arbitration, as well as rules for selecting arbitrators. Your clause should specify the rules you'll use, particularly if your chosen association has more than one set. "Arbitration will proceed according to Geriatric Judges' standard rules for commercial arbitration." See also the third example in the clause box (page 129). If you pick an arbitrator or association without standard rules, your ADR clause should address discovery and other procedural issues, so the parties don't find themselves litigating about arbitration procedures. (You can find various arbitration rulebooks online, but if you're not familiar with arbitration, you should consult an expert before committing to any of them.) At the very least, give the arbitrator power to define the rules: "The arbitrator will resolve any disputes regarding procedure for conducting the arbitration, including discovery."

In theory, arbitration is cheaper and faster than litigation because it involves less formal procedures and less crowded dockets. Some lawyers, however, doubt arbitration's value as a time or money saver. Probably the best I can say is that arbitration is *often* cheaper and faster. But arbitration does have three other clear advantages. First, in an arbitration, you can sometimes choose decision makers with appropriate technical expertise. Juries of regular folks can make a mess of technical cases, and so can judges.

Second, an arbitration clause can require *expedited* arbitration. For instance: "The parties will submit briefs within 3 business days of selection of the arbitrator; the arbitrator will hold a hearing within 3 business days of submission of briefs; and the arbitrator will issue the decision within 5 business days of the hearing." Also, ADR associations often provide procedures for expedited arbitration. So the clause might read: "In the event that the arbitration relates to release of source code for the Mission Critical Application, arbitration will proceed pursuant to Geriatric Judges' *Expedited Arbitration Rules,* and the parties will take all required actions as promptly as reasonably possible."

Third, in many countries overseas, it's easier to enforce an arbitrator's ruling than an American court's (or any foreign court's). That's because of the 1958 UN Convention on the Recognition and Enforcement of Foreign Arbitral Awards, also known as the New York Convention. The New York Convention is a treaty signed by most industrial nations, including India, China, Russia, Japan, Canada, most European countries, and the United States. Each nation promises to enforce foreign arbitrators' decisions— even though it might not always enforce foreign *courts'* decisions. Imagine you want disputes resolved in the United States, but one of the parties is Indian and has few American assets. If you litigate and win in the United States, you might need an Indian court to enforce the judgment. In most cases, you'll face fewer obstacles if that judgment came from an American arbitrator, as opposed to a U.S. court, thanks to the New York Convention. So if your contract does involve foreign interests, you should consider an arbitration clause. And if you do choose such a clause, you should mention the Convention, just to be sure everyone recognizes its role: "This Agreement is subject to the operation of the 1958 United Nations Convention on the Recognition and Enforcement of Foreign Arbitral Awards."

Finally, note that in nonnegotiable form contracts, it's usually a good idea to "call out" the arbitration clause. (That's not necessary with mediation or escalation.) The point is to warn the other party, in clear, bold text, that the contract requires arbitration. Many form contracts provide a warning on the top line: "Terms of Service: CONTAINS ARBITRATION CLAUSE." Some online contracts go even further: the link to the contract includes an arbitration warning, and a Web surfer has to click on the warning to see the contract. The reason is that courts often won't enforce an arbitration clause without clear, undeniable notice—despite the clause's "mandatory" language. (Courts are particularly hesitant to enforce arbitration on unwilling consumers.)[48]

•   •   •   •

---

48. For more on execution of form contracts, see Appendix 4.

Another type of alternate dispute resolution clause crops up in IT contracts, though it's rare. Sometimes, the parties waive their right to a jury trial. Disputes go to court, but the judge decides the facts. (In jury trials, the jury decides the facts while the judge interprets the law.) Juries tend to be more emotional than judges and less capable of grasping technical issues, so trial-by-judge has some advantages. Here's a sample jury waiver clause—in caps, to make sure no one fails to notice this waiver of constitutional rights: "EACH PARTY HEREBY WAIVES ITS RIGHT TO A TRIAL BY JURY FOR DISPUTES ARISING OUT OF OR RELATED TO THIS AGREEMENT, INCLUDING WITHOUT LIMITATION COUNTERCLAIMS REGARDING SUCH DISPUTES, CLAIMS RELATED TO THE PARTIES' NEGOTIATIONS AND INDUCEMENTS TO ENTER INTO THIS AGREEMENT, AND OTHER CHALLENGES TO THE VALIDITY OR ENFORCEABILITY OF THIS AGREEMENT. THE WAIVER IN THE PRECEDING SENTENCE APPLIES REGARDLESS OF THE TYPE OF DISPUTE, WHETHER PROCEEDING UNDER CLAIMS OF CONTRACT OR TORT (INCLUDING NEGLIGENCE) OR ANY OTHER THEORY."

T. Term and Termination

Termination clauses address four issues. First, when, if ever, will the contract expire? What is its *term* or duration? Second, when can a party terminate for cause? Third, when, if ever, can a party terminate for convenience: for any reason or no reason? Fourth, what happens after termination?

Some contracts don't need term and termination provisions. In a simple purchase agreement, for example, termination might not make sense. The provider provides the goods, and then the deal is done. There's nothing to terminate. Term and termination clauses make the most sense in contracts with continuing rights or obligations—like most software licenses and IT services contracts.

1. Term

The term is the period during which the contract operates: its duration. The word implies something temporary, like a senator's "term" of office.

In some contracts, the parties' rights and obligations continue indefinitely. In that case, use an open-ended term, continuing until someone terminates, as in the first and last examples in the clause box below. The parties can also select a more definite end date—one year from signing, for instance, or upon completion of services—as in the second and third examples in the clause box.

Term clauses often authorize one or both parties to extend the term. If the term can be extended indefinitely, it should require both

---

Term

This Agreement will continue until terminated by either party as specifically authorized herein.

•   •   •   •

This Agreement will terminate on Recipient's acceptance of the Final Deliverable (as defined in Section __).

•   •   •   •

This Agreement will remain in effect for _____ years from the date of execution by both parties. Thereafter, it will renew for successive 1 year periods, unless either party refuses such renewal by written notice 30 or more days before the end of the current term.

•   •   •   •

This Agreement will continue until terminated by either party as specifically authorized herein. Provider will provide Maintenance for a period of _____, starting at the end of the Warranty Period. Thereafter, Maintenance will renew every _____, unless Recipient notifies Provider of its intent not to renew ___ or more days before any renewal date. After Maintenance has renewed _____ times, Provider may refuse any subsequent renewal by written notice _____ days before the next renewal date.

---

parties' consent, so no one is forced into a never-ending deal. See the third example in the clause box.[49]

A term clause may address the duration of certain rights and obligations, rather than the duration of the whole contract. In software licenses, for instance, the recipient's license rights may continue indefinitely while the provider's maintenance obligations eventually end, or at least could end. In that case, the agreement has an open-ended term, but maintenance doesn't. See the last example in the previous clause box.

2. Termination for Cause

Termination for cause happens when something's gone wrong, particularly when someone's breached the contract.

The usual *cause* for termination is breach of contract. Some clauses clarify that the breach must be "material," as in the first and second examples in the following clause box. That means a minor breach, like delivering software a day late, will not authorize termination. The law generally reaches the same conclusion, but there's no harm in clarity.

Often, termination for breach clauses require advance notice—thirty days is common—and an opportunity to cure, as in the first two examples in the following clause box. If the breaching party fixes the breach during the cure period, the contract isn't terminated. But a cure period isn't required. Nor is advance notice, though the clause should at least require written notice. Also, some contracts lift the notice and cure requirement where the contract already provides a deadline for the breached obligation, or where "cure" would make no sense. If the recipient has thirty days to pay but the provider can't terminate until thirty days after notice of breach, the recipient effectively has sixty days to pay: an abuse of the cure period. And some breaches can't be cured. If the contract requires that the provider keep a secret, and the provider gives the secret to the press, thirty days to cure won't help. See the second example in the following clause box.

---

49. The third and fourth examples in the clause box are automatic renewal or "evergreen" clauses. Some states won't enforce these clauses against consumers, in some circumstances. In those cases, the contract might be considered month-to-month after the first term.

Termination for Cause

Either party may terminate this Agreement for material breach by written notice, effective in 30 days unless the other party first cures such breach.

• • • •

Either party may terminate this Agreement for material breach on 30 days' written notice with opportunity to cure; provided termination will become effective immediately upon such notice, without opportunity to cure, if: (a) this Agreement provides a specific date or period for performance of the obligation breached; or (b) the injury caused by the breach is of a type that cannot be materially reduced by the breaching party during the cure period.

• • • •

Either party may terminate this Agreement for cause by written notice, without opportunity to cure, in the event that: (a) the other party fails to function as a going concern; (b) a receiver, trustee, or other custodian for the other party or its assets is appointed, applied for, or consented to; (c) the other party becomes insolvent or unable to pay its debts as they mature in the ordinary course; (d) the other party makes an assignment for the benefit of creditors; or (e) the other party is liquidated or dissolved, or any proceedings are commenced by or against it under any bankruptcy, insolvency, or debtor's relief law.

Sometimes the parties need the right to terminate for cause even without a breach. Either party might want to escape if the other goes bankrupt, as in the third example in the clause box. (Bankruptcy will threaten payment, provision of services, and other obligations.) Other causes allowing termination for cause could include the departure of a key employee or the end of a relationship with an important third party. Often, these other *causes* don't require advance notice or an opportunity to cure.

3. *Termination for Convenience*

Termination for convenience is an escape hatch. It lets a party get out for any reason or no reason at all. If you're afraid the contract might become burdensome—including because of some business change you can't predict—consider a termination for convenience clause.

Convenience clauses sometimes authorize termination "for any reason or no reason." See the first example in the clause box below. That's arguably a clearer way of putting it, but I think "convenience" is so widely understood that the two are interchangeable.

Most convenience clauses require a notice period, as in both examples in the clause box below. Usually, that period lasts longer than the thirty days typically required in a termination for breach clause.

Many contracts impose a price on termination for convenience. The party terminating has to pay a fee. The fee generally represents a rough guess at the other party's losses caused by termination. For instance, in a services contract, the provider might spend time and money hiring or reassigning staff to serve the recipient's needs, at substantial cost. If the recipient terminates early, the termination clause could require fees that more or less match that cost. Or in a software license, the recipient might rely on the software, only to have it taken away when the provider terminates for convenience. The early termination fee would compensate the recipient for the dislocation caused by the loss of the software. See the second example in the clause box below.

Termination for Convenience

Either party may terminate this Agreement for any reason or no reason on ___ days' advance written notice.

•   •   •

Recipient may terminate this Agreement for convenience upon ___ days' advance written notice. On the date of such termination, Recipient will pay Provider an early termination fee of ___ % of the fees for Services not yet performed.

Don't confuse early termination fees with liquidated damages, covered in Chapter II.Q. Termination for convenience is not breach of contract. It's authorized. So the fee isn't a damages calculation. It's the *contract price* for early termination. Liquidated damages, on the other hand, are a species of *damages for breach* of contract. They have nothing to do with termination for convenience.

4. Effects of Termination

Termination doesn't mean the contract disappears—that it becomes null and void. In fact, termination *triggers* certain clauses. They go into effect the moment the contract terminates. Other clauses continue in force both before and after termination. So what does termination do? It ends the flow of goods and services (usually the obligations addressed in the transactional clauses, described in Part I of this book). In a software license, the recipient usually loses its rights to exploit the software. In a services contract, the provider no longer has to provide the services. And of course, the recipient doesn't have to pay for software or services it's not receiving.

Termination can trigger a variety of obligations. For instance, in some contracts, each party should promise to return the other's property upon termination, including the other party's confidential information. And as explained in Subchapter 3, termination for convenience may trigger an obligation to pay early termination fees. Some of these "triggered provisions" will already appear in other clauses. Nondisclosure clauses, for instance, typically provide: "Upon termination of this Agreement, the Receiving Party will return all Confidential Information to the Disclosing Party."[50] The termination clause often lists some of the triggered provisions too, as in the example in the following clause box.

Certain other rights and obligations "survive" termination, though they're not triggered by termination. What if the nondisclosure clause requires protection of confidential information for three years? That obligation shouldn't end just because the contract terminates after nine months. Clauses that govern interpretation of the contract generally survive too. These include provisions about alter-

---

50. See Subchapter II.H.3.

Effects of Termination

Upon termination of this Agreement, the licenses granted in Section __ (*Software License*) will terminate, Recipient will cease all use of the Software and delete all copies in its possession or control, and each party will promptly return any property of the other's. The following provisions will survive termination of this Agreement: (a) any obligation of Recipient to pay for Software used or services rendered before termination; (b) Sections __ (*Nondisclosure*), __ (*Data Security*), __ (*Indemnity*), __ (*Limitation of Liability*), and __ (*Arbitration*); and (c) any other provision of this Agreement that must survive termination to fulfill its essential purpose.

nate dispute resolution, limitations of liability, definitions, and severability.

Many contracts specify the clauses that survive termination. Often, the clause itself addresses survival: "The provisions of this Section 8 will survive any termination or expiration of this Agreement." The termination clause may also list the surviving clauses, as in the example in the clause box above. It's not strictly necessary to specify survival of clauses that govern interpretation of the contract. It should be obvious that a definitions clause or a limitation of liability clause survives. But the rule is less obvious for survivors that require affirmative action on one party's part, like indemnity and nondisclosure clauses. In general, the safest course is to specify all the clauses that survive. And just to make sure you didn't miss anything, throw in "any other provision of this Agreement that must survive to fulfill its essential purpose," as in the example in the clause box.

Software licenses raise some special termination issues. IT professionals generally assume software rights terminate with the contract, but the law isn't clear on this point. Just to be safe, providers should make sure the contract specifies license termination and explicitly requires that the recipient stop *using* the software—or the distributor stop distributing it. See the example in the clause box above. Of course, sometimes the parties do intend license survival. If the license is perpetual and irrevocable, the termination clause should list the license as one of the clauses that survives termination.[51] Also, in a value-added reseller agreement, the distributor may need to keep its rights to reproduce and use the software to the extent necessary to support its product.[52]

U. Everything Else

What have the parties negotiated? Whatever the terms are, write them in clear, simple English. As the Introduction explains, good contracts are customized. Contract drafting is a creative process, like doing business itself, so don't hesitate to blaze new trails. Just think through what you're trying to say, then write it down.

---

51. Warning: you may need to read this twice. A perpetual license should survive the term of the contract, but it ends if someone terminates. An irrevocable license should survive any termination, but it ends when the term ends. And a license that is both perpetual and irrevocable should survive the term and any termination. Make sure your termination clause reflects that structure. See Subchapter I.C.2.

52. See Subchapter I.B.1 ("Distribution").

PART THREE

Supporting Clauses

The supporting clauses include terms many professionals call "boilerplate," as well as introductory material like recitals and definitions. These clauses usually generate less debate than the general clauses and transactional clauses. But that doesn't necessarily make them less important. You can't tell what issue will crop up in a contractual relationship, so you never know when one of these supporting clauses will become vital.

The descriptions don't include clause boxes. Most, however, start with a reference to the full-length contract in Appendix 1. Look there for examples of these clauses.

A. Introduction and Recitals

See Appendix 1, first two paragraphs, page 157.

A contract's introduction generally identifies the parties and the contract itself. The recitals explain why the parties are doing business and sometimes give a little of their history. Neither introduction nor recitals is absolutely necessary. The contract's first line could read: "BluntCo, LLC will provide the following services to Laconic Industries, Inc. . . ." But recitals generally make the contract easier to understand.

The introduction and recitals should include no operative clauses: no promises, no rights, and no obligations. They might define a few terms, but otherwise they're just introductory.

The last sentence of the recitals, however, often does include some almost-operative language. It states that the contract has "consideration" or "adequate consideration." Consideration means something is exchanged: the document doesn't record a one-way transaction, like a gift. A court won't enforce an agreement without consideration. A recital's claim of consideration doesn't guarantee a court will agree, but it can help.[1]

Many recitals start with "whereas" and end with "now, therefore." For instance: "WHEREAS, Provider distributes software that makes modern writing read like a medieval charter; and WHEREAS Recipient wishes to add some flair to its otherwise dull and poorly written texts; NOW, THEREFORE, in consideration for the promises set forth below, the parties hereto agree as follows . . ." These "whereas" and "therefore" terms actually do serve a purpose. They identify the recitals, so the reader knows they're introductory, as opposed to operative clauses. But there's an easier way. Just slap the word "Recitals" above the recitals, and the words "Terms and Conditions," or just "Terms," above the rest of the contract.

---

1. Consideration lies outside the scope of this book. If you're concerned that your deal lacks consideration—lacks a two-way exchange—consult an experienced IT contracts attorney.

B. Definitions

See Appendix 1, Section 1, page 159.
If a contract uses a defined term in a single clause, it's fine to define the term in that clause. But if several sections use a defined term, readers might have trouble finding it if it's buried in Section 9. So it's often a good idea to collect all the defined terms used in more than one section and put them in a single definitions clause. That clause is usually Section 1 and lists the defined terms in alphabetical order. Like all contract terms, definitions should be as simple and clear as possible.

C. Time Is of the Essence

If a contract says "time is of the essence," even the slightest delay by either party is a material breach, at least in theory. In reality, almost no one intends such a harsh rule, so the clause's meaning requires guesswork. Which of the parties' deadlines absolutely must be met, and which don't? Because the clause is so vague, you should generally leave it out. If time is critical for some action, the contract should say so: "Any failure of Provider to deliver the Mission Critical Module on or before its due date constitutes a material breach of this Agreement." (The example in Appendix 1 does not include a time clause.)

D. Independent Contractors

See Appendix 1, Subsection 14(b), page 171.
An independent contractor clause confirms that the parties aren't partners, in the legal sense. They haven't formed a partnership. They also aren't principal and agent or employer and employee. The point is to avoid the tax implications and other legal consequences that can flow from "dependent" relationships, and to make sure neither party can make legal commitments on the other's behalf.

In services deals, the independent contractor clause should also confirm that the provider's employees won't be considered employees of the recipient, and that the provider will be responsible for all such employees' benefits and pay.

E. Choice of Law and Jurisdiction

See Appendix 1, Subsection 14(g), page 172.

A choice of law clause picks the state whose laws will govern the contract. The clause usually also picks the courts with jurisdiction over disputes. The latter choice is crucial because fighting a case downtown is easier than fighting a thousand miles away. In most cases, each party tries for the courts closest to home, or closest to its lawyers. Ideally, you'll pick the same state's law, because that's easier to manage. But it's actually possible to pick New York law and Alabama courts. Keep in mind, though, that courts are more likely to honor your decision if you choose a state with a reasonable relationship to your deal.[2]

If you don't make a choice in the contract, courts will choose for you—selecting the law and court with the closest connection to the deal. (If the recipient is a consumer, that's likely to be the recipient's home state.) If the parties hail from different states (and neither is a consumer), it's often hard to say which a court will choose. So a choice of law clause reduces uncertainty.

Some choice of law clauses disqualify two particular laws: the 1980 United Nations Convention on Contracts for the International Sale of Goods (the UN Convention) and the Uniform Computer Information Transactions Act (UCITA). The UN Convention governs some contracts between parties in different nations. Clauses like the example in Appendix 1 exclude it because the parties want Wyoming law or Texas law or whatever, and they don't want to think about whether the UN Convention applies. UCITA, on the other hand, is a purely American affair. It's a proposed law that had a lot of people up in arms a few years back. Recipients in particular felt UCITA unfairly limited their rights and remedies. Only Maryland and Virginia have adopted UCITA, but many recipients and providers exclude it, just in case their state ever does adopt it—though further spread is unlikely—or in case their deal somehow comes under a UCITA state's jurisdiction. "This Agreement will not be governed

---

2. If you have an arbitration clause or some other alternate dispute resolution procedure, the choice of law clause tells the arbitrator what law to apply. And the jurisdiction part of the clause determines what court will enforce the arbitrator's decision. See Chapter II.S.

by the Uniform Computer Information Transactions Act as adopted in any jurisdiction." The example in Appendix 1 does not address UCITA. (Some states have gone so far as to enact "bomb shelter laws": statutes that forbid application of UCITA to their citizens.)[3]

F. Notices

See Appendix 1, Subsection 14(a), page 171.
A notices provision provides an address for each party to receive notices related to the contract. With a notices clause, the parties have a legally effective address for a termination or other actions requiring notice. If the party receiving notice moves without telling the other party, and a notice doesn't get through, the termination or whatever is still effective. The failure to communicate is the receiving party's own fault.

Many notice provisions, like the example in Appendix 1, provide a system for notices. Notices will be considered received, whether they actually were or not, if sent by certified mail or whatever other mechanism the notice clause chooses.

G. Government Restricted Rights

Federal regulations give the U.S. government some surprising rights to software. If a federal agency has software developed, or receives it under certain other circumstances, it gets "unlimited license rights." The agency can make as many copies as it wants, share the software with other federal agencies and with the public, etc. Obviously, this could cost the provider a lot of sales. So providers of commercial software, or of any software not created for the feds, often include a clause addressing federal rights. The clause clarifies that the soft-

---

3. UCITA was a 1990s attempt to fix the Uniform Commercial Code (the UCC): the 1950s commercial law adopted by most states. The UCC doesn't fit IT very well. The American Law Institute, a prestigious legal advisory body, recently tried again. It recommended a set of laws and legal conclusions called *Principles of the Law of Software Contracts*. Like UCITA, the *Principles* are very controversial. No one knows whether courts or legislatures will adopt them. (For more on the *Principles*, see footnote 30 in Subchapter II.J.4 ("Disclaimers of Warranties") and footnote 33 in Subchapter II.K.1 ("Indemnity Obligation").)

ware *is not* subject to unlimited rights. Rather, it's commercial software, licensed with "restricted rights."

Government restricted rights clauses sometimes appear in standard contract forms—forms used for both government and nongovernment deals. So even if you're not working on a federal contract, you may run into a clause like the following example. If you're the recipient and you don't plan to share the software with the feds, the clause shouldn't restrict you in any important way. (Many clauses do require that you leave various notices on the software and its packaging.) And if you're the provider and you see *no* chance of distribution to the federal government, you don't need the clause. Some providers, however, include it just in case.

If you're a provider and you *are* licensing to the federal government, or to distributors who might do so, add a government restricted rights clause. But first consider consulting an attorney who specializes in government contracting and who also knows IT. (A government contracts attorney can also help you place proper government restricted rights notices in your software and on its packaging—and can help with state government contracts too.)

The example contract in Appendix 1 doesn't include a government restricted rights clause. The following, however, is sample language: "The Software is provided with Restricted Rights. Use, duplication, or disclosure for or by the government of the United States, including without limitation any of its agencies or instrumentalities, is subject to restrictions set forth, as applicable: (i) in subparagraphs (a) through (d) of the *Commercial Computer Software-Restricted Rights* clause at FAR 52.227-19; (ii) in subparagraph (c)(1) (ii) of the *Rights in Technical Data and Computer Software* clause at DFARS 252.227-7013; or (iii) in similar clauses in other federal regulations, including the NASA FAR supplement. The contractor or manufacturer is _____. Recipient will not remove or deface any restricted rights notice or other legal notice appearing in the Software or on any packaging or other media associated with the Software. Recipient will require that its customers, distributors, and other recipients of the Software agree to and acknowledge the provisions of this Section ___, in writing."[4]

---

4. "FAR" refers to the Federal Acquisition Regulations. "DFARS" refers to the Defense Federal Acquisition Regulations. And some clauses use a third set of initials, "CFR," for the Code of Federal Regulations.

H. Technology Export

See Appendix 1, Subsection 14(e), page 172.
U.S. law restricts the export of certain technologies, particularly encryption software, which has military and intelligence uses. To avoid liability to the government, software providers often require that customers promise to obey those laws. The example in Appendix 1 is a simple clause, where the recipient promises to obey all U.S. export laws and regulations. If the recipient has distributors or sublicensees, the clause should go further: "Recipient will require that all its distributors, sublicensees, customers, and other recipients of the Software sign a written agreement promising to comply with all applicable U.S. laws and regulations related to export of the Software." Some providers go even further and require an indemnification from the recipient. If the recipient breaches the export laws, it will indemnify the provider against any government or other lawsuit.[5]

Of course, foreign laws also address technology export. If the provider is concerned about a particular country, it should have an attorney licensed there prepare the clause. An international "catch-all" clause may also provide some protection: "Recipient will not export or transmit the Software across any national boundary except in compliance with all applicable laws and regulations, including without limitation the export laws and regulations of the originating country."

Providers of sensitive technology, however, shouldn't rely on contract clauses for protection. They should become familiar with export laws and seek legal advice on steps to prevent illegal export.

I. Assignment

See Appendix 1, Subsection 14(f), page 172.
An assignment clause states whether a party may transfer the contract—with all its rights and obligations—to someone else. The clause can forbid all assignments, or let only one party assign

---

5. See Chapter II.K ("Indemnity").

the contract, or permit any assignment. Many clauses, like the example in Appendix 1, permit assignment only in case of a merger.[6]

J. Force Majeure

See Appendix 1, Subsection 14(d), page 172.
A force majeure clause says the parties are not responsible for their contractual obligations if acts of God or other forces out of their control interfere. A court might reach the same conclusion, but the clause removes doubt.

K. Severability

See Appendix 1, Subsection 14(h), page 172.
A severability clause limits the impact of an unenforceable clause. It confirms that the parties intend the contract to operate as written to the maximum extent possible. They don't want the deal to fall apart, or partially fall apart, if one or more clauses can't be enforced.

Clauses like the example in Appendix 1 also try to preserve the contract, as written, by having each party waive any legal rights that would prevent full enforcement. The waiver itself might not be enforceable, but it's worth a shot.

L. No Waiver

See Appendix 1, Subsection 14(c), page 171, and Subsection 1(a), page 159.
Big companies sometimes fail to notice when someone has breached one of their contracts. So they often include a no-waiver clause. This clause provides that a party's failure to sue quickly will not waive its right to do so—and failure to respond to one breach doesn't waive the right to respond to another.

---

6. This chapter refers to assignments of an entire contract, not of intellectual property. For IP assignments, see Chapter I.D.

No-waiver clauses also tend to require that any waiver be in writing. The point is to make sure a careless oral statement by an employee doesn't waive an important contract right. But prohibitions against oral waiver aren't always enforceable, so it's a good idea to add a second layer of protection. The no-waiver clause should provide that only an authorized representative can waive a contract right. For more on authorized representatives, see Subchapter S.

M. Bankruptcy Rights

See Appendix 1, Subsection 14(i), page 172.
If a company goes bankrupt, it can escape most of its contractual obligations. Promises to provide services may be out the window, along with warranty obligations, indemnity obligations, and almost everything else. Software recipients, however, can choose to preserve their license rights. That's because Section 365(n) of the U.S. Bankruptcy Code[7] gives them that right. A bankruptcy rights clause confirms that the license is subject to Section 365(n). Confirmation isn't always necessary—Section 365(n) should protect the recipient either way—but it helps to be sure. (If the contract has a separate license section for source code or other technology in escrow, the bankruptcy rights clause should reference that section too, as does Subsection 14(i) in Appendix 1. See also Chapter II.G.)

N. Conflicts among Attachments

See Appendix 1, Subsection 14(j), page 173.
Many contracts include one or two attachments, and contracts for complex deals can include many more. What happens if the terms of these attachments contradict each other or contradict the contract's main body? What if the main body says the provider owns the deliverables, and Attachment B says the recipient owns them?

You'd think a little care would eliminate this risk. But you can't predict every possible interpretation of the contract. Plus, some

---

7. 11 U.S.C. § 365(n).

attachments could be forms attached to the contract without a lot of thought. And others, like statements of work, may be drafted after contract execution—possibly by someone who didn't read the contract. So a conflicts clause can prevent a lot of trouble.

Most clauses simply provide that, in the event of conflict, the main body overrides the attachments—as in the example in Appendix 1. That doesn't address the issue of conflicts among the other attachments, so some go further and create a complete order of precedence. For instance: "In the event of any conflict among the various exhibits to this Agreement and this main body, the following order of precedence will govern, with lower numbers overruling higher ones: (1) this main body of this Agreement; (2) any Statement of Work, with more recent Statements of Work taking precedence over later ones; (3) Exhibit A; (4) Exhibit B; and (5) Exhibit C."

Don't let the conflicts clause become an excuse for sloppy drafting. You should still review every attachment and eliminate conflicting terms.

O. Execution in Counterparts

See Appendix 1, Subsection 14(k), page 173.
Often, the parties can't get together in the same city to sign the contract. So they sign separate copies of the signature page, or of the whole document, and exchange them by fax, mail, e-mail attachment, etc. The counterparts clause says that these separate copies form a single contract.

If you execute in counterparts, make sure each party signs exactly the same document—and make sure you can prove it.[8]

P. Construction

See Appendix 1, Subsection 14(l), page 173.
Courts generally construe unclear terms against the party that wrote them. In other words, if one party wrote the contract (e.g., a clickwrap), a court will construe or interpret vague terms in a way that favors the *other* party. Construction clauses seek to eliminate that

---

8. For execution of form contracts without signature, see Appendix 4.

rule. The parties agree that there will be no favoritism in construction.

Q. Internet-Related Boilerplate

If you're an online provider, federal and state statutes may require that you include certain disclosures in your contract or on your website. For example, the federal Communications Decency Act requires that you include something like the following in your contract: "Pursuant to 47 U.S.C. Section 230(d), Provider hereby notifies Recipient that parental control protections (such as computer hardware, software, or filtering services) are commercially available that may assist in limiting access to material that is harmful to minors. Information regarding providers of such protections may be found on the Internet by searching 'parental control protection' or similar terms." Other required disclosures may address topics like data privacy[9] and consumers' right to submit complaints to the provider or to the state government.

These disclosure requirements vary from industry to industry and state to state, so if you're doing business online, you should do some research or consult with an experienced IT attorney.

R. Entire Agreement

See Appendix 1, Subsection 14(m), page 173.
The entire agreement or "integration" clause confirms that all terms the parties meant to include are *in* the agreement. It voids any letters, discussions, side agreements, or anything of that kind existing before the contract was signed, or on the day of signature.

It's important to clarify that neither party relied on any earlier or same-day communication, to help defeat any claim that one party tricked the other into signing (a.k.a. "fraud in the inducement").

---

9. See also Appendix 5's discussion of online privacy policies.

S. Amendment

See Appendix 1, Subsection 14(n), page 173, as well as Subsection 1(a), page 159.

An amendment clause lays down rules for amending the contract. Usually, it says the contract can't be amended except through a written document signed by both (or all) parties. That reduces the chance of "accidental amendment" through stupid oral promises. But prohibitions against oral amendment aren't always enforceable, so it's a good idea to add further protection against stupid promises, by providing that only the parties' authorized representatives can amend the contract. Some contracts leave it at that, without defining "authorized representative." In those agreements, the clause probably rules out interns, receptionists, and messengers, but it's hard to be sure who else. So consider a definition like: "A party's 'Authorized Representative' is any employee of that party with a title of Director or Corporate Counsel, or with a title more senior than either of those." (That assumes you've got a traditional title structure, so it's easy to determine seniority.) You can also choose a particular officer or officers, but then you have to address what happens if those positions are vacant. The same problem arises if you designate an authorized representative by name.

Designation of authorized representatives doesn't guarantee that no one else will be able to amend the contract. If a company lets an employee act like an authorized representative, a court may treat him or her that way. But designation in a contract will help.

Appendices

Sample Contracts

This appendix provides a full-length contract form. You can find an electronic version of that form at this book's website: **www.Tech ContractsHandbook.com** The website also provides an electronic library that includes other contract forms, as well as the sample language in this book's longest clause boxes.

Here are the full-length forms in the website's electronic library as of this printing:

- Standard End User Software License/EULA
- Standard Distributor Software License
- Software License and Integration Services Agreement—also printed on page 159
- License and Master Services Agreement (multiple statements of work)
- Online Terms of Service, Software as a Service
- Confidentiality and Assignment Agreement (NDA + work product assignment)
- Nondisclosure Agreement (NDA)

If you use any form provided through this book or its website, consider it no more than a starting point. A generic form will *always* need adjustment to fit a deal. Review the form carefully, compare it to the terms of your planned deal, and revise as necessary.

Also, you should be aware that this book's forms try to strike a balance between providers' and recipients' needs. So if you use one of the forms, you might want to *slant* it in your favor—or find a form that's already appropriately slanted. Form contracts used by software and services vendors generally favor the provider. They have narrow warranties and indemnities—or none at all—broad limitations of liability, strict payment terms, etc. Forms used by IT recipients generally feature broad warranty and indemnity clauses, strict delivery deadlines, etc.

If your company signs a lot of software and services contracts, consider making your own standard form, possibly using one of this book's forms as a starting point. Ideally, you would have a standard contract that doesn't need much revision for each new deal.

Finally, if you can afford it, have an experienced attorney review your contract. This book's goal is to make you as self-sufficient as possible, but as the introduction explains, there's no substitute for an attorney, or for a more experienced colleague, if you are an attorney. An experienced attorney's help is particularly important if you're creating a standard form for use in multiple deals. For the price of one contract's worth of attorney time, you can apply legal expertise to most of your deals.

●   ●   ●   ●

The following is a printed version of one of the forms listed: the Software License and Integration Services Agreement. It's a combination contract: a sale of both software and services. Software deals and services deals represent the bulk of IT contracts, so by covering both, the form gives you a broad view of the IT world.

Sample Contract

SOFTWARE LICENSE AND INTEGRATION SERVICES AGREEMENT

This Software License and Integration Agreement (this "Agreement") is entered into as of _____, 20__ (the "Effective Date") by and between _____, a _____ ("Recipient"), and _____, a _____ ("Provider").

RECITALS

Provider provides a software application known as _____ (the "Base Application"), and the parties have agreed that Provider will modify the Base Application to fit certain needs of Recipient. The parties have also agreed that Provider will provide maintenance and support services related to such modified software. Therefore, in consideration of the mutual covenants, terms, and conditions set forth below, including those outlined on Attachments A, B, and C (which are incorporated into this Agreement by this reference), the adequacy of which consideration is hereby accepted and acknowledged, the parties agree as follows.

TERMS AND CONDITIONS

1. Definitions

(a) "Authorized Representative" refers to _____ _____.

(b) "Documentation" refers to the standard end user manual for the Base Application as modified by Provider pursuant to this Agreement.

(c) "Facility" refers to Recipient's facility located at _____ _____.

(d) "Maintenance" refers to maintenance of the Software so that it performs materially in accordance with the Specifications. Maintenance includes, without limitation, the tasks listed in Part II of Attachment A.

(e) "Software" refers to the Base Application as modified by Provider pursuant to this Agreement. The Software does not include source code.

(f) "Specifications" refers to the Software technical specifications attached to this Agreement as Attachment B.

(g) "Upgrades" refers to new versions, updates, and upgrades of the Software (including without limitation of the Base Application) released commercially.

(h) "Warranty Period" refers to the _____ period following Acceptance (as defined in Section 4).

2. Services

(a) *Customization & Integration.* Provider will: (i) design and develop the Software so that it performs materially in accordance with the Specifications; and (ii) write the Documentation. Provider will provide the services required in this Subsection 2(a) on the schedule set forth in Part I of Attachment A.

(b) *Maintenance.* Provider will provide Maintenance during the term set forth in Subsection 13(a) below. Any bug fixes or other modifications of the Software created pursuant to this Subsection 2(b) will become part of the Software and will be subject to the provisions of Section 3 below and the other provisions of this Agreement.

(c) *Training.* During the term of this Agreement, Provider will provide such training on use of the Software as Recipient may reasonably request, at the Facility, without additional charge. The parties will negotiate in good faith regarding the time(s) of such training.

3. License

(a) *Grant of Rights.* Effective upon receipt of the Final Milestone payment listed in Subsection 6(a) below, Provider grants Recipient a nonexclusive license to reproduce and use the Software as necessary for Recipient's internal business purposes, provided Recipient complies with the restrictions set forth in Subsection 3(b) below. Such internal business purposes do not include use by any parent, subsidiary, or affiliate of Recipient, or any other third party, and Recipient will not permit any such use.

(b) *Restrictions.* Copies of the Software created or transferred pursuant to this Agreement are licensed, not sold, and Recipient receives no title to or ownership of any copy or of the Software itself. Furthermore, Recipient receives no rights to the Software other than those specifically granted in this Section 3. Without limiting the generality of the foregoing, Recipient will not: (i) modify, create derivative works from, distribute, publicly display, publicly perform, or sublicense the Software; (ii) use the Software for service bureau or time-sharing purposes or in any other way allow third parties to exploit the Software; or (iii) reverse engineer, decompile, disassemble, or otherwise attempt to derive any of the Software's source code.

4. Delivery & Acceptance

Provider will install the Software in the Facility on or before _____ days after the Effective Date ("Delivery"). The Software will be considered accepted ("Acceptance") (a) when Recipient provides Provider written notice of acceptance or (b) ___ days after Delivery, if Recipient has not first provided Provider with written notice of rejection. Recipient may reject the Software only in the event that it materially deviates from the Specifications. In the event of such rejection, Provider will correct the deviation and redeliver the Software within ___ days. Redelivery pursuant to the previous sentence will constitute another Delivery, and the parties will again follow the acceptance procedures set forth in this Section 4, except that after any subsequent failure of the Software to perform according to the Specifications, either party may terminate this Agreement by written notice (up until such time as the parties agree to continue the acceptance procedures of this Section 4). In the event of such termination, Provider will promptly refund all amounts paid pursuant to this Agreement, as Recipient's exclusive remedy, and Recipient will promptly return all copies of the Software.

5. Updates & Upgrades

During the term of Maintenance pursuant to Subsection 13(a) below, Provider will provide Recipient with copies of all Upgrades without additional charge, promptly after commercial release. Upon delivery to Recipient, Upgrades will become part of the Software and will be subject to the provisions of Section 3 above and the other provisions of this Agreement.

6. Payment

(a) *Development Services & License.* Recipient will pay Provider the following amounts, each subject to invoice upon the milestones listed in Part I of Attachment A:

- Milestone 1: $_____.

- Milestone 2: $_____.

- Final Milestone: $_____.

(b) *Maintenance.* For Maintenance, Recipient will pay Provider $_____ per _____, due __ days before the start of each Maintenance term, as set forth in Subsection 13(a) below. After __ Maintenance terms, Provider may increase the price for each subsequent Maintenance term by __ %, by written notice delivered ____ or more days before the renewal date.

(c) *Expenses.* Recipient will reimburse Provider for reasonable out-of-pocket expenses incurred by Provider and its employees and contractors in provision of the Services.

(d) *Invoices.* Provider will submit itemized invoices to Recipient for the payments required in this Section 6, and all invoices will be due and payable within 30 days.

7. Source Code Escrow

(a) *Escrow Agreement.* Concurrent with execution of this Agreement, the parties will execute a third party escrow agreement in the form attached hereto as Attachment C (the "Escrow Agreement"), in conjunction with _____ (the "Escrow Agent").

(b) *Deposit.* Promptly after receipt of the Final Milestone payment listed in Subsection 6(a) above, Provider will deposit with the Escrow Agent, pursuant to the procedures of the Escrow Agreement, the source code for the Software, as well as the Documentation and names and contact information for each programmer involved in creation of the Software. Promptly after release of any patch, bug fix, or other revision created pursuant to Maintenance, and promptly after release of any Upgrade, Provider will deposit updated source code, documentation, names, and contact information with the Escrow Agent. ("Deposit Material" refers to material required to be deposited pursuant to this Subsection 7(b).)

(c) *Verification.* At Recipient's request and expense, the Escrow Agent may at any time verify the Deposit Material, including without limitation by compiling source code, running tests to compare it to the Software, and reviewing the completeness and accuracy of any and all material. In the event that the Escrow Agent informs Recipient that the Deposit Material does not conform to the requirements of Subsection 7(b) above: (i) Provider will promptly deposit conforming Deposit Material; and (ii) Provider will reimburse Recipient for subsequent verification of the new Deposit Material (except to the extent that subsequent verification exceeds the cost of the unsuccessful verification by more than __ %). Any breach of the provisions of Subsection 7(c)(i) above will constitute material breach of this Agreement, and no further payments will be due from Recipient until such breach is cured, in addition to such other remedies as Recipient may have.

(d) *License & Use.* Provider hereby grants Recipient a license to use, reproduce, and create derivative works from the Deposit Material, provided Recipient may not distribute or sublicense the Deposit Material or make any use of it whatsoever except for such internal use as is necessary to maintain and support the Software. Copies of the Deposit Material created or transferred pursuant to this Agreement are licensed, not sold, and Recipient receives no title to or ownership of any copy or of the Deposit Material itself. The

Deposit Material constitutes Confidential Information of Provider pursuant to Section 11 (*Nondisclosure*) of this Agreement (provided the provisions of Subsection 11(d) calling for return of Confidential Information before termination of this Agreement will not apply to the Deposit Material).

(e) *Release Conditions.* The term "Release Conditions," as used in the Escrow Agreement, refers to any of the following: (i) material breach by Provider of Subsection 2(b) of this Agreement, if such breach remains uncured ___ or more days after Recipient's written notice; (ii) any failure of Provider to function as a going concern; (iii) appointment, application for, or consent to a receiver, trustee, or other custodian for Provider or its assets; (iv) Provider becomes insolvent or unable to pay its debts as they mature in the ordinary course or makes an assignment for the benefit of creditors; or (v) Provider is liquidated or dissolved, or any proceedings are commenced with regard to Provider under any bankruptcy, insolvency, or debtor's relief law.

8. Warranties

(a) *Function.* Provider warrants that, during the Warranty Period, the Software will perform materially as described in the Specifications. In the event of breach of the warranty in this Subsection 8(a), Provider will promptly repair the Software or replace it with software of substantially similar functionality. The remedies set forth in this Subsection 8(a) are not exclusive of any others Recipient may have.

(b) *Infringement/Ownership.* Provider warrants that it is the owner of the Software and of each and every component thereof, or the recipient of a valid license thereto, and that it has and will maintain the full power and authority to grant the intellectual property and other rights granted in this Agreement without the further consent of any third party. If the Software becomes, or in either party's reasonable opinion is likely to become, the subject of any claim, suit, or proceeding arising from or alleging infringement of any intellectual property right, or in the event of any adjudication that the Software infringes any such right, Provider, at its own expense, will promptly take the following actions: (i) secure for Recipient the right to continue using the Software; or (ii) replace or modify the Software to make it non-infringing, provided such modification or replacement will not materially degrade any functionality relied upon by Recipient. The remedies set forth in the preceding sentence are not exclusive of any others Recipient may have at law or in equity.

(c) *Harmful Code.* Provider warrants that the Software and any media used to distribute it contain no viruses or other computer instructions or technological means intended to disrupt, damage, or interfere with the use of computers or related systems.

(d) *Services Performance.* Provider warrants that all services provided pursuant to this Agreement will be performed in a workmanlike manner.

(e) *Right to Do Business.* Each party warrants that it has the full right and authority to enter into, execute, and perform its obligations under this Agreement and that no pending or threatened claim or litigation known to it would have a material adverse impact on its ability to perform as required by this Agreement.

(f) *Disclaimers.* EXCEPT FOR THE EXPRESS WARRANTIES SPECIFIED IN THIS SECTION 8, PROVIDER MAKES NO WARRANTIES, EITHER EXPRESS OR IMPLIED, INCLUDING WITHOUT LIMITATION ANY IMPLIED WARRANTIES OF MERCHANTABILITY OR FITNESS FOR A PARTICULAR PURPOSE. Provider does not warrant that the Software will perform without error or that it will run without immaterial interruption. Provider provides no warranty regarding, and will have no responsibility for, any claim arising out of: (i) a modification of the Software made by anyone other than Provider, unless Provider approves such modification in writing; or (ii) use of the Software in combination with any operating system not authorized in the Documentation or Specifications or with hardware or software specifically forbidden by the Documentation or Specifications. The warranty in Subsection 8(b) above does not apply to the extent that the infringement arises out of any of the conditions listed in Subsection 9(d) below.

9. Indemnity

(a) *Indemnified Parties & Claims.* The "Indemnified Parties" are Recipient and its officers, directors, shareholders, parents, subsidiaries, agents, insurers, successors, and assigns. An "Indemnified Claim" is any third party claim, suit, or proceeding against the Indemnified Parties arising out of, related to, or alleging: (i) infringement of any patent, copyright, or other intellectual property right by the Software; or (ii) injury to or death of any individual, or any loss of or damage to real or tangible personal property, caused by the negligence of Provider or of any of its agents, subcontractors, or employees.

(b) *Indemnity.* Provider will indemnify, defend, and hold the Indemnified Parties harmless against any Indemnified Claim, provided Recipient gives Provider prompt notice of such Indemnified Claim. Provider's obligations set forth in the preceding sentence include, without limitation, retention and payment of attorneys and payment of court costs, as well as settlement at Provider's expense, payment of judgments, or both.

(c) *Litigation.* Provider will control the defense of any Indemnified Claim, including appeals, negotiations, and any settlement or compromise thereof; provided Recipient will have the right to approve the terms of any settlement or compromise that restricts its rights granted under this Agreement or subjects it to any ongoing obligations.

(d) *Exclusions.* Provider's obligations set forth in Subsection 9(b) above do not apply to the extent that a Subsection 9(a)(i) Indemnified Claim arises out of:

(i) Recipient's violation of this Agreement;

(ii) revisions to the Software made without Provider's written consent;

(iii) Provider's modification of the Software in compliance with technical specifications provided by Recipient, or in compliance with a method or process provided by Recipient for implementing such specifications, unless Provider knew of the potential infringement at the time of such modification and did not notify Recipient;

(iv) Recipient's failure to incorporate Software updates or upgrades that would have avoided the alleged infringement, provided Provider offered such updates or upgrades without fees or charges not otherwise required pursuant to this Agreement;

(v) use of the Software in combination with hardware or software not provided by Provider: (A) that is specifically forbidden by the Documentation or Specifications; or (B) that is not designated in the Documentation or Specifications as available for interface with the Software, unless such hardware or software is necessary for the Software to perform a function listed in the Documentation or Specifications.

10. Limitation of Liability

(a) *Limitations.* Except as provided below in Subsection 10(b): (i) IN NO EVENT WILL PROVIDER'S LIABILITY ARISING OUT OF OR RELATED TO THIS AGREEMENT EXCEED $_____; AND (ii) IN NO EVENT WILL PROVIDER BE LIABLE FOR ANY CONSEQUENTIAL, INDIRECT, SPECIAL, INCIDENTAL, OR PUNITIVE DAMAGES. THE LIABILITIES LIMITED BY THIS SUBSECTION 10(a) APPLY: (A) TO LIABILITY FOR NEGLIGENCE; (B) REGARDLESS OF THE FORM OF ACTION, WHETHER IN CONTRACT, TORT, STRICT PRODUCT LIABILITY, OR OTHERWISE; (C) EVEN IF PROVIDER IS

ADVISED IN ADVANCE OF THE POSSIBILITY OF THE DAMAGES IN QUESTION AND EVEN IF SUCH DAMAGES WERE FORESEEABLE; AND (D) EVEN IF RECIPIENT'S REMEDIES FAIL OF THEIR ESSENTIAL PURPOSE. If applicable law limits the application of the provisions of this Subsection 10(a), Provider's liability will be limited to the maximum extent permissible.

(b) *Exclusions.* Subsection 10(a) above does not apply to (i) claims pursuant to Section 9 or (ii) claims for attorneys' fees and other litigation costs Recipient becomes entitled to recover as a prevailing party in any action.

11. Nondisclosure

(a) *Confidential Information.* "Confidential Information" refers to the following items one party to this Agreement (the "Disclosing Party") discloses to the other (the "Receiving Party"): (i) any document the Disclosing Party marks "Confidential"; and (ii) any information the Disclosing Party orally designates as "Confidential" at the time of disclosure, provided the Disclosing Party confirms such designation in writing within ___ business days. Notwithstanding the foregoing, Confidential Information does not include information that: (A) is in the Receiving Party's possession at the time of disclosure; (B) is independently developed by the Receiving Party without use of or reference to Confidential Information; (C) becomes known publicly, before or after disclosure, other than as a result of the Receiving Party's improper action or inaction; or (D) is approved for release in writing by the Disclosing Party.

(b) *Nondisclosure Obligations.* The Receiving Party will not use Confidential Information for any purpose other than to facilitate the provision of service pursuant to this Agreement (the "Purpose"). The Receiving Party: (i) will not disclose Confidential Information to any employee or contractor of the Receiving Party unless such person needs access in order to facilitate the Purpose and executes a nondisclosure agreement with the Receiving Party, with terms no less restrictive than those of this Section 11; and (ii) will not disclose Confidential Information to any other third party without the Disclosing Party's prior written consent. Without limiting the generality of the foregoing, the Receiving Party will protect Confidential Information with the same degree of care it uses to protect its own confidential information of similar nature and importance, but with no less than reasonable care. The Receiving Party will promptly notify the Disclosing Party of any misuse or misappropriation of Confidential Information that comes to the Receiving Party's attention. Notwithstanding the foregoing, the Receiving Party may disclose Confidential Information as required by applicable law or by proper legal or governmental authority. The Receiving Party will give the Disclosing Party prompt notice of any such legal or governmental demand and reasonably cooperate with the Disclosing Party in any effort to seek a protective order or otherwise to contest such required disclosure, at the Disclosing Party's expense.

(c) *Injunction.* The Receiving Party agrees that breach of this Section 11 might cause the Disclosing Party irreparable injury, for which monetary damages would not provide adequate compensation, and that in addition to any other remedy, the Disclosing Party will be entitled to injunctive relief against such breach or threatened breach, without proving actual damage or posting a bond or other security.

(d) *Termination and Return.* The obligations of Subsection 11(b) above will terminate _____ after the Effective Date. Upon termination of this Agreement or upon the Disclosing Party's written request, the Receiving Party will return all copies of Confidential Information to the Disclosing Party or certify, in writing, the destruction thereof.

(e) *Retention of Rights.* This Section 11 does not transfer ownership of Confidential Information or grant a license thereto. Except to the extent that another section of this Agreement specifically provides to the contrary, the Disclosing Party will retain all right, title, and interest in and to all Confidential Information.

12. Arbitration

Any claim arising out of or related to this Agreement, including without limitation claims related to the parties' negotiations and inducements to enter into this Agreement, will be submitted to mandatory, binding arbitration under the auspices of _____ (the "Arbitration Association"), in _____, with the parties sharing equally the costs of arbitration. Arbitration will proceed according to the standard _____ rules of the Arbitration Association. This Section 12 does not limit either party's right to provisional or ancillary remedies from a court of competent jurisdiction before, after, or during the pendency of any arbitration, and the exercise of any such remedy does not waive either party's right to arbitration. Judgment on an arbitration award may be entered by any court with competent jurisdiction.

13. Term & Termination

(a) *Term.* This Agreement will continue until terminated by either party as specifically authorized herein. Provider will provide Maintenance for a period of _____, starting upon Acceptance (as defined in Section 4). Thereafter, the Maintenance term will renew every _____, unless Recipient notifies Provider of its intent not to renew ___ or more days before any renewal date. After the Maintenance term has renewed _____ times, Provider may refuse any subsequent renewal by written notice _____ days before the next renewal date.

(b) *Termination for Cause.* Either party may terminate this Agreement for material breach by written notice, effective in 30 days unless the other party first cures such breach.

(c) *Termination for Convenience.* Recipient may terminate this Agreement for any reason or no reason upon __ days' advance written notice. On the date of such termination, Recipient will pay Provider an early termination fee calculated as follows: _____.

(d) *Effects of Termination.* Upon termination of this Agreement, the licenses granted in Sections 3 and 7(d) will terminate, Recipient will cease all use of the Software and delete all copies in its possession or control, and each party will promptly return any property of the other's. The following provisions will survive termination of this Agreement: (i) any obligation of Recipient to pay for services rendered before termination; (ii) Sections 9 through 12 of this Agreement; and (iii) any other provision of this Agreement that must survive termination to fulfill its essential purpose.

14. Miscellaneous

(a) *Notices.* Notices pursuant to this Agreement will be sent to the addresses below, or to such others as either party may provide in writing. Such notices will be deemed received at such addresses upon the earlier of (i) actual receipt or (ii) delivery in person, by fax with written confirmation of receipt, or by certified mail return receipt requested.

For Provider: _____.

For Recipient: _____.

(b) *Independent Contractors.* The parties are independent contractors and will so represent themselves in all regards. Neither party is the agent of the other and neither may bind the other in any way. The parties agree that no Provider employee or contractor will be an employee of Recipient. Provider will be responsible for all employment rights and benefits of Provider employees, including without limitation: (i) federal, state, and local income and employment taxes and social security contributions; (ii) workers' compensation, health benefits, vacation pay, holiday pay, profit sharing, retirement, pension, disability benefits, and other health and welfare benefits, plans, or programs; and (iii) insurance.

(c) *No Waiver.* Neither party will be deemed to have waived any of its rights under this Agreement by lapse of time or by any statement or representation other than (i) by an Authorized Representative and (ii) in an explicit written waiver. No waiver of a breach of this Agreement will constitute a waiver of any prior or subsequent breach of this Agreement.

(d) *Force Majeure.* To the extent caused by *force majeure,* no delay, failure, or default will constitute a breach of this Agreement.

(e) *Technology Export.* Recipient will not export the Software or otherwise remove it from the United States except in compliance with all applicable U.S. laws and regulations.

(f) *Assignment & Successors.* Neither party may assign this Agreement or any of its rights or obligations hereunder without the other's express written consent, except that either party may assign this Agreement to the surviving party in a merger of that party into another entity. Except to the extent forbidden in the previous sentence, this Agreement will be binding upon and inure to the benefit of the respective successors and assigns of the parties.

(g) *Choice of Law & Jurisdiction.* This Agreement will be governed solely by the internal laws of the State of _____, without reference to: (i) such State's principles of conflicts of law; (ii) the 1980 United Nations Convention on Contracts for the International Sale of Goods; or (iii) other international laws. The parties consent to the personal and exclusive jurisdiction of the federal and state courts of _____, _____.

(h) *Severability.* To the extent permitted by applicable law, the parties hereby waive any provision of law that would render any clause of this Agreement invalid or otherwise unenforceable in any respect. In the event that a provision of this Agreement is held to be invalid or otherwise unenforceable, such provision will be interpreted to fulfill its intended purpose to the maximum extent permitted by applicable law, and the remaining provisions of this Agreement will continue in full force and effect.

(i) *Bankruptcy Rights.* The rights and licenses granted to Recipient in Sections 3 and 7(d) of this Agreement are licenses to "intellectual property" rights, as defined in Section 365(n) of the United States Bankruptcy Code (11 U.S.C. Section

101, *et seq.*). If Provider is subject to any proceeding under the United States Bankruptcy Code, and Provider as debtor in possession or its trustee in bankruptcy elects to reject this Agreement, Recipient may, pursuant to 11 U.S.C. Section 365(n)(1) and (2), retain any and all of the rights granted to it under Sections 3 and 7(d) of this Agreement to the maximum extent permitted by law. This Subsection 14(i) will not be construed to limit or restrict any right or remedy not set forth in this Subsection 14(i), including without limitation the right to retain any license or authority this Agreement grants pursuant to any provision other than Sections 3 or 7(d).

(j) *Conflicts among Attachments.* In the event of any conflict between the terms of this main body of this Agreement and those of any attachment, the terms of this main body will govern.

(k) *Execution in Counterparts.* This Agreement may be executed in one or more counterparts. Each counterpart will be an original, but all such counterparts will constitute a single instrument.

(l) *Construction.* The parties agree that the terms of this Agreement result from negotiations between them. This Agreement will not be construed in favor of or against either party by reason of authorship.

(m) *Entire Agreement.* This Agreement sets forth the entire agreement of the parties and supersedes all prior or contemporaneous writings, negotiations, and discussions with respect to the subject matter hereof. Neither party has relied upon any such prior or contemporaneous communications.

(n) *Amendment.* This Agreement may not be modified except (i) by Authorized Representatives of each party and (ii) in a written contract signed by both parties.

[signature block]
—*page break*—

Attachment A: Services Description

Part I: Customization & Integration Schedule & Milestones

[insert]

Part II: Maintenance & Support Tasks

[insert]
—*page break*—

Attachment B: Specifications

[insert]
—*page break*—

Attachment C: Escrow Agreement

[insert]

Copyrights, Patents, and Other Intellectual Property Rights

This appendix provides a brief explanation of intellectual property, a field of law important to many IT transactions, particularly licenses.

Intellectual property law lets creators monopolize certain products of their intellect. Because of IP law, you can *own* an invention you've developed. You can also own software or a story you've written, a photograph you've taken, a sculpture you've carved, a name or logo you've used in commerce, and various other types of intangible property. And your ownership covers more than just your physical products. If you build a better mousetrap and get a patent, you own more than the mousetraps you manufacture. You can monopolize the invention itself so that no one else can build mousetraps based on your design. If you write a story, you own more than the copies you print; you can keep anyone else from printing and selling your story, because of your copyright. In other words, if you have a patent or copyright, or benefit from one of the other forms of IP, you can monopolize the intangible products of your brain.

Companies can own intellectual property too, of course. A company can purchase IP, and companies often own IP their employees create within the scope of their duties.

Intellectual property is one of the central sources of value in the IT industry, but it's important not to exaggerate its reach. Many IT professionals assume someone owns every innovation. That's wrong.[1] In fact, you should look at intellectual property as the exception, not the rule. In U.S. law, ideas and innovations are free as the birds. If I come up with a great invention or other innovation and tell you about it, you're almost always free to exploit it. You can take my innovation and make millions, or become famous, leaving me behind. It's only in certain rare instances that I can monopolize the product of my brain. It's only if I have a patent or copyright—or if my work fits into one of the other narrow exceptions to the basic rules—that innovations belong to everyone.

Intellectual property plays a central role in technology licenses and ownership transfers. In those transactions, the license or transfer is a grant of IP rights. Most of the rest of the contract, however, has little to do with intellectual property. And in a pure technology *services* agreement—without a transfer of technology rights—IP plays no role. So intellectual property law is important to IT contracting, but it's not the only game in town.

IP consists principally of copyrights, patents, trade secrets, and trademarks. All of these rights are important to a variety of businesses, including IT companies, but only copyrights and patents play a unique role in the IT industry.

Copyright applies to any original work of authorship fixed in a tangible medium of expression—like a story written down in a book or software written on a disk. As discussed in Chapter I.C, a copyright holder has the exclusive right to reproduce (copy), modify, distribute, publicly perform, and publicly display his or her work. Software licenses generally address those rights, because copyright applies to almost all software. Copyright comes into existence at the moment of authorship, so if you write original software, you automatically own the copyright. You can register a copyright with the

---

1. This misunderstanding leads to some silly contracts. The worst offender is the "feedback" license. Two IT companies plan to collaborate, and Company A wants Company B to grant a license to all "feedback" its employees generate. The fear is that Company B will suggest a new marketing strategy for Company A, or come up with some other feedback on Company A's business, and Company A won't be able to use the feedback because of Company B's IP rights. Balderdash. Company A will be perfectly free to use Company B's marketing idea or other feedback. Company B would only have IP rights in the rare instance where it develops a patentable invention. Even then, Company A could use the invention unless and until Company B files a patent application, goes through the patent process, and actually gets a patent issued. It might make sense to write a license to patents Company B generates as a result of the project—if Company B is willing to give up rights to future patents of unknown value—but it makes no sense to license feedback.

U.S. Library of Congress, and registration helps enforce your rights. But registration isn't necessary for ownership. Duration of copyright varies, but generally copyright lasts seventy years from the death of the author, or one hundred and twenty years from creation in the case of a corporation authoring software through its employees.[2]

Copyright applies to expression—to written words, written software, etc.—not to the underlying ideas or inventions. So if you write a book about computer repair, copyright gives you the exclusive right to reproduce and distribute that book. It doesn't give you exclusive rights to your computer repair *techniques*. An imitator could read your book and use your techniques to start a competing computer repair business. Your imitator could even write his own computer repair book, laying out techniques learned in your book—so long as he doesn't reproduce the actual words of your book. The same goes for software. An imitator can read your source code—the human-readable version of your software—and write her own software using your ideas and techniques. (That's why so many companies keep their source code secret.) That's generally perfectly legal, so long as the imitator doesn't copy any of the actual code. If you want to protect a technique or process or design built into your software—other than by keeping it secret—copyright won't help you. For that, you need a patent.

A patent is a government grant of certain rights to a device or process—to an invention. To get a patent, you have to apply to the U.S. Patent and Trademark Office (the PTO). The PTO will only grant the patent if the invention meets certain criteria. It has to be "novel, useful, and nonobvious." If you do get a patent, you have exclusive rights to make the invention or have it made, and to use, market, sell, offer for sale, and import it. Those monopoly rights generally continue for twenty years.[3]

Some software includes patented processes—patented inventions. But end users and distributors generally don't need patent licenses for that software. A copyright license will grant all the necessary rights, even to patented software. That's why software contracts rarely cover patent rights (and this book only addresses them briefly, in Chapter I.D).

---

2. Copyright is governed by the Copyright Act of 1976, 17 U.S.C. § 101 *et seq.* Mask works—a close relative of copyright (defined in the Mini-Glossary)—are governed by the Semiconductor Chip Protection Act of 1984, 17 U.S.C. § 902 *et seq.*

3. Patent law is governed by the Patent Act, 35 U.S.C.

Open Source Software Contracts

An open source contract grants the recipient access to the software's source code. It also permits modification of the software and redistribution of both the original and the new, modified version. At least, that's a thumbnail explanation of a complex concept. This appendix explains open source contracts. All such contracts are copyright license agreements, so you'll understand this appendix better if you first read Chapter I.C ("Software Licenses in General").[1]

"Open source" is often confused with "free," but open source software isn't necessarily free. Providers can charge for open source software, so long as they don't charge any additional fee or royalty for source code or for the rights to modify and redistribute. But because each customer can redistribute the software—at any price or no price—market forces usually keep providers from charging a lot. If the price is high, customers can just get the software from someone else: from another recipient. As a result, much open source software actually is free, and most is relatively inexpensive. Some providers don't care about making money. Others make money by charging for related services, like maintenance and consulting.

"Open source" is also often confused with "public domain," and that's also a mistake. If software is in the public domain, it's entirely free of copyright and other intellectual property restrictions. No one needs a license to copy it, and we're all free to modify it, distribute new versions, etc. Open source software, on the other hand, is licensed

---

1. For a more complete definition of "open source," see *The Open Source Definition* provided by the Open Source Initiative: http://www.opensource.org/docs/osd.

by definition. So it's governed by copyright law. The license just grants some freedoms that aren't common in commercial licenses—along with some unique restrictions, in many cases.

The key advantage of open source software is *evolution*. When the source code is widely available and developers are free to fix bugs, add new modules, and otherwise revise, the software improves. If the various improvements circulate, recipients will choose the best ones and use and redistribute those. So software quality increases through natural selection. Compare that to typical commercial in-house development. A small group of developers tests and improves the software during a limited period, possibly with help from some beta customers. No one else's input finds its way into the code.

But the open source model comes with some disadvantages for commercial software providers. As discussed, each recipient can redistribute the software and compete with the provider, limiting license revenues. Also, source code often includes sensitive techniques, and revealing it shares those techniques with competitors. Finally, some open source licenses include additional restrictions that can cause problems for commercial developers. See the following for these "copyleft" or "viral" restrictions. As a result, many providers won't invest a lot of resources in creating open source software, with potential impacts on quality.

Software providers rarely draft their own open source licenses. They license software under standard form agreements widely used in the open source community. Among other reasons, open source recipients prefer familiar terms, as opposed to contracts they'd have to scrutinize. (That's ironic because some of the widely used forms have unclear terms and unanswered questions about enforceability.) So this appendix doesn't offer proposed language for open source contracts. It does, however, refer you to some of the best-known open source contract forms.

The rest of this appendix explains the two most common types of open source software license clauses. It also briefly describes the nonlicensing terms that generally appear in open source form contracts.

Copyleft/Viral Licenses

"Copyleft" is a flavor of open source licensing that turns copy*right* protection around. Copyleft license terms govern more than a single transaction, where the provider licenses software under the open source model. Copyleft requires that the recipient *also* use the open source model, if it redistributes the software. In fact, copyleft requires that *all* future recipients of the software use the open source model if they redistribute.

Imagine a developer recipient creates a "derivative work" of copyleft software: it modifies the software to create a new application or adds the software to a larger application. If the developer distributes one of these derivative works, it has to use the open source model. It has to distribute the new application with source code and with the right to modify and redistribute. In other words, if copyleft software gets into another application, it "infects" that application, turning it into open source software. That's why copyleft licenses are called "viral" open source licenses.

Not surprisingly, copyleft licenses are unpopular with many commercial developers. In fact, copyleft creates a nightmare scenario for developers: an engineer includes a small amount of copyleft-licensed software in a massive application, without telling anyone. Now the whole application is "infected": it's all open source software. Even worse, the developer's customers face the same problem. If they create a derivative work by combining the infected software with any of their own applications, they catch the open source virus too, and have to treat their own application as open source software. The result could be the loss of millions of dollars invested in commercial software, and a thicket of lawsuits.

At least, that's the concern. It's rarely actually happened. And the courts have yet to enforce the core copyleft provisions, so it's not clear that they're enforceable.

The best-known copyleft license is the GNU General Public License (the GPL), provided by the Free Software Foundation, a non-profit dedicated to the open source model. You can find the most current edition of the GPL, version 3, online at http://www.gnu.org/licenses/gpl.html. The key copyleft licensing provisions appear in Sections 2, 4 through 6, and 10. But version 3 is relatively new, and most software licensed under the GPL uses version 2, found at http://

www.gnu.org/licenses/gpl-2.0.html. In version 2, look in particular at Sections 1 through 3. Whatever version you review, beware: the GPL is not for the faint of heart. The language confuses many lawyers—including me—so don't be surprised if you have to read it over and over.

If you're a recipient and all you want to do is *use* the software, copyleft licensing shouldn't worry you. In fact, you'll probably benefit from the software "commons" created by copyleft: from the fact that other recipients contribute new code to a community of developers, for use by all. The same goes for recipients who plan to distribute but don't mind sharing source code and letting others redistribute their applications. Copyleft doesn't present a problem. However, if you plan to distribute and you want to keep your source code to yourself, or if you want to make sure no one else can distribute your application, *don't* include copyleft software. In fact, in that case you should insist that your providers do everything possible to exclude copyleft software from *their* products, and protect you from the consequences if some slips in anyway. Among other remedies, you should consider an open source warranty in your contracts with providers, as well as a strong intellectual property indemnity.[2]

Less Restrictive Open Source Licenses

Copyleft licensing is common, but there are many alternatives. In fact, most open source licenses lack copyleft provisions. They let the recipient include open source software in a larger application and then distribute that application under a traditional commercial software license—without using the open source model.

The BSD-type licenses are the least restrictive open source contracts. The category is named for the Berkeley Software Distribution of Unix, an open source operating system. These contracts place no IP restriction on redistribution of software.

The BSD category includes several contracts, including the BSD License itself, as well as the MIT License, named for the Massachusetts Institute of Technology. You can find current versions of both the BSD and MIT licenses online at the website of the Open Source Initiative, another open source nonprofit. Both licenses are short

---

2. See Subchapter II.J.3 ("Other Warranties") and Chapter II.K ("Indemnity").

and easy to read. The BSD License appears at http://www.open source.org/licenses/bsd-license.php, and the MIT License appears at http://www.opensource.org/licenses/mit-license.php.

The Mozilla Public License is slightly more restrictive but still widely viewed as friendly to commercial software developers. It's maintained by the Mozilla Foundation, yet another open source nonprofit (and the source of the Firefox browser). Like copyleft forms, the Mozilla license requires that modified versions of the software be distributed under the open source model: with source code and with the right to modify and redistribute. But that restriction is far narrower (and clearer) than the copyleft restriction. It doesn't apply to all derivative works—just to "modifications" of the original code: to individual files that contain the original software. So if the recipient puts the open source software into a larger application, it hasn't "infected" the whole application. It has to use the open source model for the files containing the original open source software, but it can distribute the rest of the application under any IP terms it likes.

You can find the Mozilla Public License at http://www.mozilla .org/MPL/MPL-1.1.html. It's longer than the BSD and MIT licenses, but the language is relatively manageable. In version 1.1, see in particular Sections 1.9, 2, 3.1, 3.2, 3.6, and 3.7.

Other Terms of Open Source Contracts

Open source contracts generally include various disclaimers and notice requirements. A disclaimer of functionality and other warranties is almost universal. Open source software is usually provided "as is," without warranties (express or implied).[3] And warranty disclaimers go hand in hand with notice requirements. The provider doesn't want downstream recipients—those who get the software directly or indirectly from the original recipient—to expect warranties either. So when the recipient redistributes the code, it's required to include the warranty disclaimer. Generally, recipients also have to include copyright notices, informing downstream recipients that the software is subject to copyright and identifying the copyright holder.

---

3. See Chapter II.J ("Warranty").

Other terms are less universal. Open source contracts may include limitations of liability, patent licenses (with "open" terms similar to the copyright licenses discussed previously), government restricted rights clauses, and choice of law clauses, among other provisions.[4]

---

4. See respectively, Chapter II.L ("Limitation of Liability"), Appendix 2 ("Copyrights, Patents, and Other Intellectual Property Rights"), and Chapters III.G ("Government Restricted Rights") and III.E ("Choice of Law and Jurisdiction").

Clickwraps, Browsewraps, and Other Contracts Executed without Ink

This appendix covers contracts that aren't signed in ink: usually nonnegotiable standard agreements prepared by the provider of products or services, or of a website. The main issue is enforceability. If you're the provider, you've got to make sure your recipient executes the contract in a way that confirms both notice of the terms and consent. Without notice and consent, you don't have a binding contract, and a court won't enforce its terms.

The first part of this appendix addresses initial execution and the second addresses amendment.

Execution

We traditionally confirm notice and consent through an ink signature. Courts enforce signed contracts because we're all expected to know what a signature means. If you signed on the dotted line and didn't realize you'd consented to the terms above that line . . . well, that's your problem.

Obviously, an ink signature isn't always practical for a form contract. That's where shrinkwrap contracts come in, along with clickwraps and browsewraps. These signature alternatives work if they confirm notice of the contract's terms and consent to those terms.

A *shrinkwrap* contract is a printed form accompanying a product container. It might be printed on the outside of a box of software, or it might be a paper form held against the box by a plastic wrapper. The name "shrinkwrap," in fact, comes from the clear, plastic, shrink-to-fit wrappers traditionally used with these contracts. A shrinkwrap generally begins with something like: "By opening this box, you agree to the contract terms below." The recipient confirms notice of the terms and consent by opening the box. If the recipient reads the terms and doesn't consent, he or she doesn't open the box and can return the product for a full refund.

Courts have accepted the logic of notice and consent by shrinkwrap, so they'll usually enforce the contract. But notice and consent have to be meaningful. If the contract isn't clearly visible—if the recipient might open the box without noticing—a court might refuse enforcement. Courts might also refuse if the recipient can't easily return the product after reading the full contract. If you're the provider, you have to accept returns from recipients who didn't like the shrinkwrap terms. And you can't set up a burdensome return process. Also, remember that consent isn't meaningful until *after* full notice of the terms. If you don't put the whole contract outside the box, *opening* the box can't be the last step in contract execution. Instead, the shrinkwrap might read: "By installing the software enclosed in this box, you consent to the terms below."

A *clickwrap* contract is an electronic form posted online or on a start-up screen of a software application. It says something like: "By clicking 'I agree' below, you agree to the following terms." The recipient can't install the software or use the service until he or she clicks "I agree." And some clickwraps go further: the recipient can't click "I agree" until he or she scrolls all the way through the contract.

If you use a clickwrap, make sure the "click" comes before payment—or at least make sure the recipient can easily return the software if he or she decides not to click. If you do that, a clickwrap is better than a shrinkwrap. The recipient can't persuasively argue that he or she didn't notice the contract or understand that consent was necessary.

A *browsewrap* contract is an online form without a click-to-agree feature. For instance, many websites provide a "terms of service" link at the bottom of each page. The recipient doesn't have to click "I agree" or take any other action to use the site or the products or services provided there.

You'll find browsewraps harder to enforce than clickwraps or shrinkwraps, because it's harder to establish notice and consent. The recipient might not notice the contract or realize it applies to him or her (or care). So you should avoid browsewraps if possible, and use clickwraps.

Sometimes, however, a clickwrap isn't practical. No one clicks "I agree" to surf a website. If you have to use a browsewrap, give the recipient clear notice of the terms and of the fact that they apply to him or her. Ideally, you'd splash big flashing letters across the top of each webpage: "BY USING THIS WEBSITE, YOU CONSENT TO THE TERMS AND CONDITIONS POSTED HERE." That's almost never practical, but keep it in mind as the ideal, and make your notice as visible as possible. Also, if you're offering a product or service that requires some action by the recipient, the notice should immediately precede the action point. For instance, just above a software download button, provide a link reading: "DO NOT CLICK THE DOWNLOAD BUTTON BELOW UNLESS YOU AGREE TO THE TERMS AND CONDITIONS POSTED HERE." Of course, once you've gone that far, you might as well use a clickwrap.

Some contracts are *hybrids*: both clickwrap and browsewrap. Many websites require that their paying customers sign up online, and in the process click "I agree" to contract terms. That's a clickwrap. These sites also provide a link to the same contract at the bottom of each page, for website visitors who never sign up. It's the same contract, but now it's a browsewrap. If you use a hybrid, keep in mind that you're less likely to enforce it against casual visitors— against browsewrap recipients—than against clickwrap customers.

Finally, whatever type of contract you use, make sure the recipient has some way to save and store the terms. That's easy enough online, because we can all print just about any webpage we come across. But providers should consider going the extra mile and making it easy. You might include a "click here to print" button, or a "click here to download a copy" button.

Within software applications (as opposed to online), access to the contract becomes more important. Few of us could track down the clickwrap we executed when we first booted up our computer. So providers should be sure to include a print or save choice for their offline clickwraps.

Unilateral Amendment

Generally, a contract can't be revised after execution unless the parties sign or click an amendment or a new version (or agree orally). But execution of an amendment or new version isn't always practical. That's where the unilateral (one-sided) amendment clause comes in. It gives the provider the right to change the agreement even if the recipient doesn't execute anything.

Unilateral amendment plays a role in ongoing services relationships, particularly ongoing relationships surrounding software as a service (SaaS) and other machine-based services.[1] It doesn't make much sense for "one night stand relationships," where the recipient executes a new contract every time it interacts with the provider.

Many services contracts include something like the following: "Provider may amend this Agreement by posting a new version at the Website, and such amendment will become effective upon posting thereof. Recipient will periodically review the Website for amendments, and Recipient's continued use of the System after an amendment will indicate consent thereto." That might once have worked, but no longer. Customers don't actually search their online contracts for revisions, and the courts consider search requirements unrealistic. So the clause fails the notice and consent test.

Unfortunately, it's not clear what kind of notice and consent an amendment clause needs because the law isn't well settled. The consequences of a mistake aren't clear either. I suspect most legal scholars would say a bad amendment clause fails to create an effective and speedy system for contract amendment but does no other harm. But at least one court has suggested that a bad clause invalidates the whole contract.[2] If that's right, a mistake might cost the provider its limitation of liability, disclaimers of warranties, payment terms, etc.

If the law gets clearer, I'll post a notice at this book's website (www.TechContractsHandbook.com). In the meantime, I think the first example in the following clause box is effective and safe. I don't think it'll invalidate contracts, and I think it's almost certainly

---

1. See Chapter I.F ("Software as a Service and Other Machine-Based Services").

2. *Harris v. Blockbuster*, 2009 WL 1011732 (N.D. Tex. 2009). The *Harris* court implied that a really bad amendment clause renders the whole contract "illusory" because the provider could change any provision at will.

Unilateral Amendment

Provider may amend this Agreement from time to time by posting an amended version at its website and sending Recipient written notice thereof. Such amendment will be deemed accepted and become effective 30 days after such notice (the "Proposed Amendment Date") unless Recipient first gives Provider written notice of rejection of the amendment. In the event of such rejection, this Agreement will continue under its original provisions, and the amendment will become effective at the start of Recipient's next Term following the Proposed Amendment Date (unless Recipient first terminates this Agreement pursuant to Section __ (*Term & Termination*)). Recipient's continued use of the Service following the effective date of an amendment will confirm Recipient's consent thereto. This agreement may not be amended in any way except through a written agreement by Authorized Representatives of each party.

• • • •

Provider may amend this Agreement from time to time by posting an amended version at the Website and sending Recipient written notice thereof. Such amendment will become effective 30 days after such notice (unless Recipient first terminates this Agreement pursuant to Section __ (*Term & Termination*)). Recipient's continued use of the Service after such 30-day notice period will confirm Recipient's consent to such amendment. This agreement may not be amended in any way except through a written agreement by Authorized Representatives of each party.

---

enforceable. THE SECOND EXAMPLE IN THE CLAUSE BOX, however, CREATES SOME RISK. So before using it, review the text below.

Obviously, unilateral amendment isn't good for recipients. They should avoid it in negotiated contracts. If the provider can change the contract later, why bother with negotiations? But for online services with standard terms, recipients usually can't avoid unilateral amendment.

• • • •

The examples in the clause box above assume the contract is posted online. If not, replace the "posting" provisions with something like: "Provider may revise this Agreement from time to time by sending a new version to Recipient."

Each example in the previous clause box requires concrete *notice* of contract amendments, like an e-mail or letter.[3] The first example also has concrete *consent* terms. It gives the recipient thirty days to review the amendment. If the recipient accepts the change, it does nothing, and the amendment becomes effective after that thirty days. If the recipient rejects the changes, it notifies the provider and the contract continues under its original provisions. But at the start of the recipient's next term, the amendment goes into effect whether the recipient likes it or not. Presumably the recipient can terminate the agreement at the start of the next term, so it can reject the amendment by walking away.[4] In other words, the first example provides for both notice and consent.

Providers could instead give recipients the right to terminate the agreement if they don't like the amendment. But most providers prefer to minimize customer termination rights. The first example gives the recipient a meaningful choice—which should make the clause enforceable—but doesn't allow early termination. Plus, in most online services, the vast majority of recipients will do nothing—they won't respond to the amendment notice—so the amendment will usually become effective in thirty days.

The second example in the clause box does *not* specifically grant the recipient a chance to reject the amendment. But if another section of the contract lets the recipient terminate for convenience relatively promptly, the clause still provides a meaningful choice. The recipient can reject the amendment by quitting the relation-

---

3. E-mail notice is far more effective than notice through a website, but it has some problems. Spam filters often block bulk e-mails, and various laws regulate e-mail, requiring opt-out mechanisms and other protections for recipients. So providers shouldn't rely on e-mail if they can help it. Letters are more reliable, of course, but not practical for many providers. RSS feeds are practical and effective, and so are Twitter messages (tweets), so providers should consider combining either or both of those with e-mail notice. ("RSS" stands for "really simple syndication" or "rich site summary," depending who you ask. Twitter can be found at www.Twitter.com.) In general, providers should consider multiple means of notice: whatever's necessary to make sure recipients get the message.

4. See Subchapter II.T.1 ("Term").

ship.[5] So consent is meaningful, and the clause should be enforceable. Just make sure the unilateral amendment clause gives the recipient enough time. If the contract's termination clause says the recipient can terminate for convenience instantly, or on ten or fifteen or twenty days' notice, the second example works. Thirty days should then be enough time to read the amended provisions, decide what to do, and give notice if the recipient wants to terminate. But if the recipient has to give thirty days' notice to terminate for convenience, the clause should give at least *forty* days before amended terms go into effect.

What if recipients *can't* terminate for convenience? Will the second example in the previous clause box work? I think the second example has three possible outcomes in that case. First, it might work just fine. Second, it might be only partially effective but do no harm. Courts might enforce it for amendment of certain provisions, particularly provisions that aren't considered fundamental to the basis of the bargain, like billing and notice procedures (as opposed to "fundamental" provisions, like prices and arbitration clauses). And even if amendments don't go into effect in thirty days, as the clause intends, they might become effective the next time the recipient renews the service or takes some other action that reaffirms its commitment.

The third possible outcome is disaster for the provider. A court might hold that the second example in the clause box invalidates the whole contract. I think that's unlikely, but providers shouldn't ignore the risk.

What about "one night stand" relationships? As noted previously, unilateral amendment makes little sense for relationships that involve a new contract every time the parties interact. If the provider intends such a relationship, it should make sure its online contract leaves no doubt. "THIS AGREEMENT GOVERNS A SINGLE INSTANCE OF ACCESS TO THE SERVICE [*or* A SINGLE DOWNLOAD OF THE SOFTWARE]. TO ACCESS THE SERVICE AGAIN, RECIPIENT MUST AGREE SEPARATELY TO PROVIDER'S THEN-CURRENT TERMS OF SERVICE, WHICH MAY OR MAY NOT MATCH THIS AGREEMENT. RECIPIENT IS ON NOTICE THAT THIS AGREEMENT DOES NOT GOVERN FUTURE

---

5. See Subchapter II.T.3 ("Termination for Convenience"). The right to terminate won't necessarily be called "termination for convenience." Some contracts simply let the recipient end the relationship at any time, on short notice.

ACCESS TO THE SERVICE AND THAT RECIPIENT MUST RE-VIEW AND ACCEPT PROVIDER'S THEN-STANDARD TERMS OF SERVICE FOR FUTURE ACCESS." Terms like that play a particularly important role in browsewrap contracts.

Everything said above applies to *contract* amendments. I think providers can amend online policy documents more easily, though the law isn't clear. (See Appendix 5 for online policy documents.) I think the following will generally work: "Notwithstanding the provisions of Subsection 13(g) (*Unilateral Amendment*), Provider may amend the Privacy Policy and Acceptable Use Policy at any time by posting a new version of either at the Website. Such new version will become effective on the date it is posted." That clause has all the faults previously discussed. But it should work if the online policy documents are separate from the contract: if they're not contract terms. And I think it might work even if the contract incorporates the policy documents. That's because online policy documents work like internal policies, which companies generally change at will, rather than like traditional contract clauses. At least, they work that way if the provider keeps fundamental contract provisions out of the online policy documents and sticks to their natural subject matter: privacy procedures, acceptable use, responses to copyright claims, etc. I think tech buyers and sellers accept the idea of amendment without advance consent for online policy documents, and the courts will follow their lead. Nothing is certain, though, so providers should consider adding a notice requirement if they do specifically incorporate online policy documents into their contracts. "Notwithstanding the provisions of Subsection 13(g) (*Unilateral Amendment*), Provider may amend the Privacy Policy and Acceptable Use Policy at any time by posting a new version of either at the Website and sending Recipient written notice thereof. Such new version will become effective 5 business days after such notice."

Online Policy Documents

This appendix covers acceptable use policies (AUPs), Digital Millennium Copyright Act (DMCA) policies, and privacy policies. Companies doing business online post these documents on their websites to explain their rules and procedures.

AUPs, DMCA policies, and privacy policies aren't exactly contract clauses. They're just statements: information for customers and other users. Still, some online policy documents work like contract clauses. When customers buy products and services online, they often rely on AUPs and privacy policies, and that can make those policies binding on the provider. Also, some online agreements require that customers comply with certain policies, particularly AUPs, while others fully incorporate all their policies into the contract, transforming them into contract clauses binding on both parties. However this incorporation issue plays out, providers should be sure to obey all their own online policies.

As you'll see, each example policy in the following clause boxes includes a "Date Posted" or "Effective Date." You should include these dates in all your online policies. They help recipients determine whether the policy has changed since they last reviewed it (assuming they ever do).

Acceptable Use Policies

AUPs outline user behavior that won't be tolerated. They're most useful for services that enable online communication. Internet service providers, for instance, should consider AUPs. So should Internet hosting companies and websites with chat rooms and space for customer postings.

As noted, the AUP is a policy statement at heart, not a contract clause. But if you're the provider, there's no reason your contract can't require compliance with your AUP. "Recipient will comply with Provider's acceptable use policy ("AUP"), posted at www.congenialme.com, as such policy may change from time to time." Just make sure incorporation of the AUP doesn't tie your hands. Retain the right to change the AUP—as authorized in the suggested language above and, usually, in the AUP itself. See part D of the example in the following clause box. And make sure incorporation into the contract doesn't require that you enforce rules you don't always want enforced, or fully enforced. "Neither this Agreement nor the AUP requires that Provider take any action against any customer or

---

AUP

Date Posted: _____

A. Unacceptable Use

Provider requires that all customers and other users of Provider's Internet service (the "Service") conduct themselves with respect for others. In particular, please observe the following rules in your use of the Service:

1) *Abusive Behavior:* Do not harass, threaten, or defame any person or entity. Do not contact any person who has requested no further contact. Do not use ethnic or religious slurs against any person or group.

2) *Privacy:* Do not violate the privacy rights of any person. Do not collect or disclose any personal address, social security number, or other personally identifiable information without each holder's written permission. Do not cooperate in or facilitate identity theft.

3) *Intellectual Property:* Do not infringe upon the copyrights, trademark rights, trade secret rights, or other intellectual property rights of any person or entity. Do not reproduce,

publish, or disseminate software, audio recordings, video recordings, photographs, articles, or other works of authorship
without the written permission of the copyright holder.

4) *Hacking, Viruses, & Network Attacks:* Do not access any
computer or communications system without authorization,
including the computers used to provide the Service. Do not
attempt to penetrate or disable any security system. Do not
intentionally distribute a computer virus, launch a denial of
service attack, or in any other way attempt to interfere with
the functioning of any computer, communications system,
or website. Do not attempt to access or otherwise interfere
with the accounts of other users of the Service.

5) *Spam:* Do not send bulk unsolicited e-mails ("Spam") or sell
or market any product or service advertised by or connected
with Spam. Do not facilitate or cooperate in the dissemina-
tion of Spam in any way. Do not violate the CAN-Spam Act
of 2003.

6) *Fraud:* Do not issue fraudulent offers to sell or buy products,
services, or investments. Do not mislead anyone about the
details or nature of a commercial transaction. Do not com-
mit fraud in any other way.

7) *Violations of Law:* Do not violate any law.

B. Consequences of Violation

Violation of this Acceptable Use Policy (this "AUP") may lead to
suspension or termination of the user's account or legal action. In
addition, the user may be required to pay for the costs of investi-
gation and remedial action related to AUP violations. Provider
reserves the right to take any other remedial action it sees fit.

C. Reporting Unacceptable Use

Provider requests that anyone with information about a violation of this AUP report it via an e-mail to the following address:
_____. Please provide the date and time (with time zone)
of the violation and any identifying information regarding the
violator, including e-mail or IP (internet protocol) address if
available, as well as details of the violation.

D. Revision of AUP

Provider may change this AUP at any time by posting a new version on this page and sending the user written notice thereof. The new version will become effective on the date of such notice.[1]

---

user violating the AUP, but Provider is free to take any such action it sees fit."

The behavior forbidden by an AUP depends on the nature of the provider's business. The example in the previous clause box would work for a variety of online communications providers. When you design your own AUP, think about user behavior that could injure you, injure your users, or lead to liability.

An AUP doesn't have to list consequences for violation, but it's usually a good idea. Your goal is to inform. Generally, consequences for violation should include suspension of the service or termination, as in part B of the previous clause box. But make sure you don't limit yourself. For instance, part B says the provider can take any other actions it sees fit.

The AUP doesn't need a reporting clause either, but you might want watchful users to help police your service. See part C of the clause box.

Finally, AUP prohibitions often include imprecise language— language you'd want to avoid in a contract, if possible. For instance, part A.5 in the previous clause box defines "Spam" as "bulk unsolicited e-mail." What does "bulk" mean? And exactly what do "harass" and "threaten" mean in part A.1? AUPs often deal with hard-to-define concepts—concepts like *respect*, which lies at the heart of every AUP. So it's hard to avoid some imprecision. But do everything you can to make your AUP clear. And when you're dealing with potential AUP violations, give the recipient the benefit of the doubt regarding unclear terms. That practice will help if you ever wind up in court, battling over whether an AUP-related termination was justified.

---

1. See the last paragraph of Appendix 4 (in the text covering "Unilateral Amendment") for contracting concerns surrounding amending online policy documents.

DMCA/Copyright Notice Policies

The Digital Millennium Copyright Act is a U.S. federal law. One of its provisions protects online communications providers from copyright liability. If an ISP or other provider follows certain procedures, it's not liable for copyright infringement initiated by its subscribers. In other words, if a subscriber posts a third party's recording or article or other copyrighted work, the *subscriber* might be liable for copyright infringement, but the provider isn't—even though the provider's computers made the unauthorized copy and displayed it to the public.[2]

DMCA policies help providers take advantage of the act's "safe harbor": its protection from liability. The policies are online announcements about the provider's procedures surrounding copyright infringement. That's why they're sometimes called "copyright notice policies" or "intellectual property infringement policies."

This appendix covers DMCA policies and related contract terms, but it doesn't go into detail about the safe harbor's other requirements. However, since some knowledge of the other requirements will help you understand DMCA policies, here's a summary. First, the safe harbor only applies if you, the provider, had no knowledge of the copyright infringement, and got no financial benefit directly attributable to infringement. Second, to take advantage of the safe harbor, you must take the following steps:

(1) Make sure your network doesn't block any technical measures copyright holders use to protect their work or to identify infringement.
(2) Designate an agent to receive copyright complaints, and register that agent's contact information with the U.S. Copyright Office.
(3) Post the agent's contact information online.
(4) Enforce a policy calling for termination of subscribers who repeatedly infringe copyrights, and inform subscribers of that policy.

---

2. The DMCA appears in multiple sections of the U.S. Code. This appendix discusses one of several portions of the DMCA, called the Online Copyright Infringement Liability Limitation Act, 17 U.S.C. § 512.

The DMCA refers to customers and other users as "subscribers," so this part of Appendix 5 uses the same term.

(5) Follow the copyright notice, take-down, and counter-notice procedures discussed below.[3]

Steps (3) and (4) are the only ones that require statements to the public or to subscribers, so they're the only ones you have to address in a DMCA policy. A provider can address them by posting something like the following:

> For claims of copyright infringement, please contact _____ [name of registered agent and/or his or her department, address, phone number, and e-mail address]. We will terminate the accounts of subscribers who are repeat copyright infringers.

That's it. You don't need more for a DMCA policy.

Many policies go further. They explain step (5): the act's "notice and take-down procedures." In short, if someone sends the provider a properly detailed notice of copyright infringement, complaining about materials posted by a subscriber, the provider promptly removes the accused materials. If the provider does that, it's not liable for copyright infringement. Of course, removing the materials might create liability to the subscriber (though not if your contract gives you the right to remove suspicious materials). But the DMCA protects the provider there too. To take advantage of that berth in the safe harbor, the provider informs the subscriber of the claim. Then, if the subscriber sends a properly detailed "counter-notice," claiming the materials don't infringe copyright, the provider puts the materials back up. If the provider does all that, it avoids liability for copyright infringement and for removing the materials. From there, the claimant and subscriber can fight it out in court, and the provider doesn't have to worry.

Most DMCA policies tell the public how to notify the provider of copyright claims. They also tell subscribers how to respond if their materials are taken down.

Much of the language in the following clause box comes directly from the Digital Millennium Copyright Act. You should

---

3. This summary isn't detailed enough to ensure full compliance. You can find various DMCA guides online, and of course a short consultation with an experienced attorney should tell you all you need. You can also read the statute (which is written in English, believe it or not).

DMCA Policy

Date Posted: _____

This policy statement lists our requirements for notice of copyright infringement and for responses to such a notice if you or your materials are accused.

We use the copyright infringement procedures of the Digital Millennium Copyright Act.

A. Notice of Copyright Infringement

To notify us of copyright infringement, please send a written communication to our Copyright Notices Department, at the contact points listed below in Part C. That written communication should include the following:

1) A physical or electronic signature of a person authorized to act on behalf of the owner of an exclusive right that is allegedly infringed.

2) Identification of the copyrighted work claimed to have been infringed, or, if multiple copyrighted works at a single online site are covered by a single notification, a representative list of such works at that site.

3) Identification of the material that is claimed to be infringing or to be the subject of infringing activity and that is to be removed or access to which is to be disabled, and information reasonably sufficient to permit us to locate the material.

4) Information reasonably sufficient to permit us to contact the complaining party, such as an address, telephone number, and, if available, an electronic mail address at which the complaining party may be contacted.

5) A statement that the complaining party has a good faith belief that use of the material in the manner complained of is not authorized by the copyright owner, its agent, or the law.

6) A statement that the information in the notification is accurate, and under penalty of perjury, that the complaining

party is authorized to act on behalf of the owner of an exclusive right that is allegedly infringed.

B. Counter-Notice by Accused Subscriber

If you are a subscriber and we have taken down your materials due to suspicion of copyright infringement, you may dispute the alleged infringement by sending a written communication to our Copyright Notice Department, at the contact points listed in Part C below. That written communication should include the following:

1) A physical or electronic signature of the subscriber.

2) Identification of the material that has been removed or to which access has been disabled and the location at which the material appeared before it was removed or access to it was disabled.

3) A statement under penalty of perjury that the subscriber has a good faith belief that the material was removed or disabled as a result of mistake or misidentification of the material to be removed or disabled.

4) The subscriber's name, address, and telephone number, and a statement that the subscriber consents to the jurisdiction of Federal District Court for the judicial district in which such address is located, or if the subscriber's address is outside of the United States, the Federal District Court for _____ [insert provider's home district], and that the subscriber will accept service of process from the person who provided notification of copyright infringement or an agent of such person.

C. Agent for Notices

Please send all notices required by this policy to our Copyright Notice Department at _____ [address, phone number, and e-mail address].

D. Termination of Repeat Infringers

In appropriate circumstances, we will terminate the accounts of subscribers who are repeat copyright infringers.

E. Revision of Policy

We may revise this policy at any time, including by posting a new version at this website.[4]

---

stick close to that language. DMCA policies don't call for a lot of creativity.

Whatever your DMCA policy says, you should post it in a prominent place on your website—ideally a page linked to your home page.

The act requires that you notify subscribers of your policy against repeat infringers. So if that notice appears in your DMCA policy—as in part D of the previous clause box—you should make sure subscribers *see* the policy. You might include a link in a sign-up screen, or just send a link early in the relationship. Or you might include something like the following in your subscriber agreement: "Subscriber is on notice that Provider may terminate the accounts of subscribers who are repeat copyright infringers."[5]

Many providers include a long DMCA policy in the body of their subscriber agreement, as a contract clause. I think that's a mistake—at least if the DMCA policy includes notice and take-down procedures, like parts A and B in the previous clause box. If you include the policy in your contract, the notice and take-down procedures are no longer optional. You *have* to follow them. What if you mishandle the procedures? A subscriber could sue you for breach of contract. You've turned an optional legal protection into a liability. Of course, you could avoid the problem by stating that the DMCA policy binds the subscriber but not you. But why bother? Including the procedures in the contract won't increase your safe harbor protection. And most copyright claimants will be third parties, not your subscribers. A contract clause wouldn't bind them, and if the DMCA policy appears in your contract, rather than a separate webpage,

---

4. See the last paragraph of Appendix 4 (in the text covering "Unilateral Amendment") for contracting concerns surrounding amending online policy documents.

5. You could also include the repeat infringer policy in your AUP. But you still have to make sure subscribers see it.

third parties might never stumble across it. That defeats the purpose.

Privacy Policies

In a privacy policy, the provider of a website or an online service explains what it will and won't do with users' private information.

In general, any website or online service that collects personally identifiable information should have a privacy policy. "Personally identifiable information" (PII) refers to any information that could be used to identify an individual, or to contact or locate an individual. That includes sensitive information, like social security numbers, credit card numbers, bank account numbers, and medical records. But it also includes more widely available information, like e-mail addresses, snail mail addresses, and telephone numbers, as well the *names* of users. So the only websites that don't need privacy policies are simple signposts—sites that collect no information—and sites that collect nothing but 100 percent anonymous feedback, like survey responses that couldn't possibly be used to identify the responder. Arguably, websites that post their operators' e-mail addresses should have privacy policies, even if they collect no information. Users could send e-mail, thus revealing personally identifiable information: their e-mail addresses.

Where does this privacy policy "requirement" come from? The United States has no unified set of laws governing privacy. Instead, we have a confusing array of federal and state statutes. And when you add European and other foreign regulations—which may govern providers serving foreign recipients—the list of laws and regulations grows. There's a fair chance that a law requiring or encouraging privacy policies applies to your site or service.[6] Even if not, you should consider a privacy policy because it can limit your liability. If you honestly and fully disclose the use you'll make of private information, users can't easily argue that they never knew about your use or authorized it. Finally, privacy policies make

---

6. Providers should consider consulting with a lawyer who handles e-commerce and privacy, to learn about applicable privacy-related laws. Privacy policies make up only one piece of the privacy puzzle. This book addresses one of the other pieces, data security, in Subchapter II.I.2, but there are many more.

business sense. They make users and business partners comfortable.

Because the United States lacks a unified privacy law, it's hard to say exactly what information should appear in your policy. As I've mentioned before, this book is no substitute for an experienced lawyer's advice. But it is possible to lay out a broad set of privacy policy best practices. In general, your privacy policy should do the following to limit legal risk:

1. Identify the categories of personally identifiable information collected.
2. Identify the categories of third parties that receive PII or have access to it (if any).
3. Describe the ways PII is used.
4. Summarize security measures to protect PII.
5. Tell users how they can review and change their PII (assuming they can).
6. Explain how you notify users of changes to the privacy policy.
7. List the policy's effective date.
8. Say nothing in the privacy policy that is not absolutely and consistently true.[7]

Is a privacy policy a contract clause? In one way, the answer is academic. If a site or service provider posts a policy, users will rely on it, and that reliance will probably render the policy binding on the provider. Various laws might also make the policy binding. Still, if you're a provider, it's generally a bad idea to specifically incorporate your policy into your contract, because it could limit your right to revise the policy without users' consent.[8]

The following clause box envisions a provider that sells products and services online, and that has customers create a "sign-in account."

---

7. Recommendations 1, 2, and 5 through 7 are required by one of the better-known state statutes on privacy policies: California's Online Privacy Protection Act of 2003, Cal. Business and Professions Code § 22575 *et seq.*—particularly § 22575(b).

8. The law on this point isn't clear. For more on this issue, see the last paragraph of Appendix 4 (in the text covering "Unilateral Amendment").

Privacy Policy

Effective Date: _____

We collect certain information through our website, located at _____ (our "Website"). This page (this "Privacy Policy") lays out our policies and procedures surrounding the collection and handling of any such information that identifies an individual user or that could be used to contact or locate him or her ("Personally Identifiable Information" or "PII").

This Privacy Policy applies only to our Website. It does not apply to any third party site or service linked to our Website or recommended or referred by our Website or by our staff. And it does not apply to any other website or online service operated by our company, or to any of our offline activities.

A. PII We Collect

We collect the following Personally Identifiable Information from users who buy our products and services: name, e-mail address, telephone number, address, and credit card number.

We also use "cookies" to collect certain information from all users, including website visitors who don't buy anything through our Website. A cookie is a string of data our system sends to your computer and then uses to identify your computer when you return to our Website. Cookies give us usage data, like how often you visit, where you go at the site, and what you do.

B. Our Use of PII

We use your Personally Identifiable Information to create your account, to communicate with you about products and services you've purchased, to offer you additional products and services, and to bill you. We also use that information to the extent necessary to enforce our Website terms of service and to prevent imminent harm to persons or property.

We use cookies so that our Website can remember you and provide you with the information you're most likely to need. For instance, when you return to our Website, cookies identify you and prompt the site to provide your username (not your password), so you can sign in more quickly. Cookies also allow our Website to remind you of your past purchases and to suggest similar products and services. Finally, we use information gained through cookies to compile statistical information about use of our Website, such as the time users spend at the site and the pages they visit most often. Those statistics do not include PII.

C. Protection of PII

We employ the following data security tools to protect Personally Identifiable Information: _____
_____. Unfortunately, even with these measures, we cannot guarantee the security of PII. By using our Website, you acknowledge and agree that we make no such guarantee, and that you use our Website at your own risk.

D. Contractor and Other Third Party Access to PII

We give certain independent contractors access to Personally Identifiable Information. Those contractors assist us with _____. All those contractors are required to sign contracts in which they promise to protect PII using procedures reasonably equivalent to ours. (Users are not third party beneficiaries of those contracts.) We also may disclose PII to attorneys, collection agencies, or law enforcement authorities to address potential AUP violations, other contract violations, or illegal behavior. And we disclose any information demanded in a court order or otherwise required by law or to prevent imminent harm to persons or property.

As noted above, we compile Website usage statistics from data collected through cookies. We may publish those statistics or share them with third parties, but they don't include PII.

E. Accessing and Correcting Your PII

You can access and change any Personally Identifiable Information we store through your "My Account" page.

F. Amendment of This Privacy Policy

We may change this Privacy Policy at any time by posting a new version on this page or on a successor page. The new version will become effective on the date it's posted, which will be listed at the top of the page as the new Effective Date.

The example in the previous clause box is bare-bones: it lacks reassuring language about the provider's respect for privacy. But you might consider adding something like: "Your privacy is important to us."

The example also lacks contact information for a privacy officer who can discuss PII. Sometimes it's a good idea to make such a person available and to post his or her contact information in the privacy policy.

The law imposes special privacy-related obligations on certain businesses, including businesses that collect medical records, financial data, and information about children.[9] Those obligations may impact the content of your privacy policy. If you operate in an industry that might be subject to special privacy regulation, you should get help from a lawyer with privacy expertise.

---

9. The federal government's key data security laws include the Gramm-Leach-Bliley Act (governing financial institutions), the Health Insurance Portability and Accountability Act, the Children's Online Privacy Protection Act, and arguably the Sarbanes-Oxley Act (on corporate corruption and financial reporting). Most states have information privacy laws too.

Mini-Glossary

Below are seven terms and phrases used repeatedly in this book's clause boxes:

calendar year, calendar month, calendar quarter: Shorthand for a period defined by the standard calendar. Calendar year is often contrasted with a company's *fiscal year*, which may not start on January 1. September is a calendar month, while "the 30 days following delivery" is a month defined by the contract. Finally, the first calendar quarter consists of January, February, and March, and the remaining three calendar quarters are likewise defined by sets of three consecutive calendar months.

including without limitation: A quick way to say: "The following is one example, but the fact that one example is listed does *not* mean there are no others." For instance, a license clause might read: "Provider will indemnify Recipient against all intellectual property claims, including without limitation claims related to the TrollTech Patent." The fact that the clause lists TrollTech patent claims doesn't mean other IP claims are left out.

machine-based service: As Chapter I.F explains, a machine-based service is a technical service provided through computers and software. These include telecommunications and Internet connectivity. They also include systems typically called "software as a service." Machine-based services are distinguished from professional services. The two overlap, but in general, professional services rely on people more than machines. (Professional services include technology consulting, software programming, tech support, etc.)

mask works: A stepsister of copyrights. Mask works are three-dimensional patterns involved in the creation of semiconductors (computer chips). They're governed by their own statute: the Semiconductor Chip Protection Act of 1984, 17 U.S.C. § 902 *et seq.* This book doesn't directly address mask works, except to the extent that they're mentioned in Appendix 2 and included in the examples in Chapter I.D ("Software Ownership: Assignment and Work-for-Hire").

object code: A version of software that a computer can read. It's also sometimes called "machine-readable code." (Actually, those two terms don't have identical meanings, but they're close enough for our purposes.) Object code is contrasted with source code.

source code: The version of software that a human programmer can read. In fact, source code is the version a human wrote: the original version of most software. Source code gets "compiled" or translated into object code.

without limiting the generality of the foregoing: A quick way to say: "The preceding text gives a broad, general rule. A specific and narrow example follows, but the fact that the example is specific and narrow does not make the general rule any less broad or general." For instance, a license clause might provide: "Distributor will exercise its best efforts to market and sell the Software. Without limiting the generality of the foregoing, if Distributor fails to achieve gross revenues of $500,000 from Software distribution during any calendar year, Provider may revoke the license granted in this Section." The rule about minimum royalties is related to the general *best efforts* rule, but it doesn't limit that rule. So the fact that the distributor hits its revenues number doesn't necessarily mean that it's complied with its "best efforts" obligation.

Additional Resources

Below are additional resources I recommend related to technology contracts. Most are directed to lawyers or law students.

Online Materials

Electronic Frontier Foundation website: http://www.eff.org/.

Eric Goldman (Santa Clara University School of Law professor) Technology Law and Marketing Blog: http://blog.ericgoldman.org/.

FindLaw.com, FindLaw for Legal Professionals, sample business contracts, technology industry: http://contracts.corporate.findlaw.com.

Law & Life: Silicon Valley (blog by attorney Mark Radcliffe): http://lawandlifesilicon valley.com/blog/.

OneCLE website, sample contracts and other resources: http://www.onecle.com/.

Open Source Initiative website: http://www.opensource.org/.

Books

Ballon, *E-Commerce & Internet Law, Treatise with Forms*, 2nd Ed. (Thomson Reuters/ West 2009).

Bro (ed.), *The E-Business Legal Arsenal: Practitioner Agreements and Checklists* (ABA Publishing 2004).

Classen, *A Practical Guide to Software Licensing for Licensees and Licensors*, 3rd Ed. (ABA Publishing 2008).

Epstein and Politano (ed.), *Drafting License Agreements*, 4th Ed. (Aspen Publishers 2010, 2003–2009).

Farnsworth, *Farnsworth on Contracts*, 3rd Ed. (Aspen Publishers 2004).

Keyes, *Government Contracts under the Federal Acquisition Regulations*, 3rd Ed. (West Publishing Co. 2003).

Index

IP Attorney's Handbook for Insurance Coverage in Intellectual Property Disputes

By David A. Gauntlett

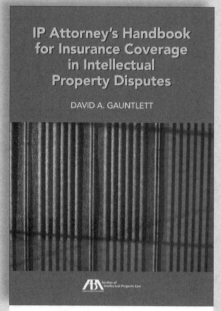

$129.95; $110.95 for ABA Members;
$103.95 for Section of Intellectual Property Law
Product Code: 5370168
© 2010

This easy-to-use guide addresses clients' questions regarding insurance coverage for intellectual property and contains vital information for intellectual property litigators who wish to use insurance to reimburse the cost of defending intellectual property lawsuits, or obtain moneys for their settlement and/or indemnification of damage awards.

The book focuses on the kind of policy language carriers have used, how courts have interpreted these, and issues intellectual property practitioners need to be sensitive to in litigating insurance cases so that they are "insurance savvy." It also highlights issues that are of particular concern to practitioners who must weave in and out of the labyrinth of insurance coverage cases that march to a distinctive set of often counter-intuitive rules.

About the Section of Intellectual Property Law

From its strength within the American Bar Association, the ABA Section of Intellectual Property Law (ABA-IPL) advances the development and improvement of intellectual property laws and their fair and just administration. The Section furthers the goals of its members by sharing knowledge and balanced insight on the full spectrum of intellectual property law and practice, including patents, trademarks, copyright, industrial design, literary and artistic works, scientific works, and innovation. Providing a forum for rich perspectives and reasoned commentary, ABA-IPL serves as the ABA voice of intellectual property law within the profession, before policy makers, and with the public.